A-Z ST

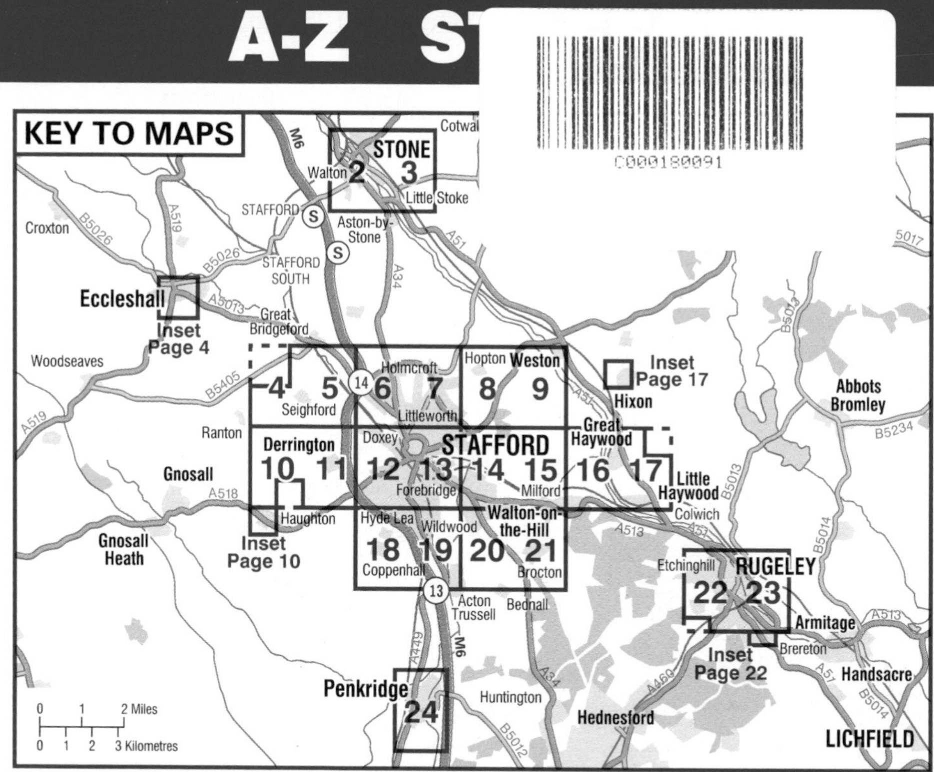

Reference

- Motorway — M6
- A Road — A513
  - Proposed
- B Road — B5066
- Dual Carriageway
- One Way Street
  Traffic flow on A roads is also indicated by a heavy line on the driver's left.
- Pedestrianized Road
- Track
- Footpath
- Residential Walkway

- Railway — Tunnel, Level Crossing, Station
- Built Up Area — WEST CL.
- Local Authority Boundary
- Posttown Boundary
- Postcode Boundary
- Map Continuation — 8
- Car Park Selected — P
- Church or Chapel — †
- Fire Station
- Hospital — H
- House Numbers A & B Roads only — 17 54
- Information Centre — i

- National Grid Reference — 325
- Police Station — ▲
- Post Office — ★
- Toilet
  - with facilities for the Disabled
- Educational Establishment
- Hospital, Hospice or Health Centre
- Industrial Building
- Leisure or Recreational Facility
- Place of Interest
- Public Building
- Shopping Centre or Market
- Other Selected Buildings

Scale 1:15,840

0 ¼ ½ Mile

0 250 500 750 Metres 1 Kilometre

4 inches (10.16 cm) to 1 mile
6.31cm to 1kilometre

Head Office:
Fairfield Road, Borough Green, Sevenoaks, Kent TN15 8PP
Telephone 01732 781000 (General Enquiries & Trade Sales)
Showrooms:
44 Gray's Inn Road, London WC1X 8HX
Telephone 020 7440 9500 (Retail Sales)
www.a-zmaps.co.uk

Edition 2 2002

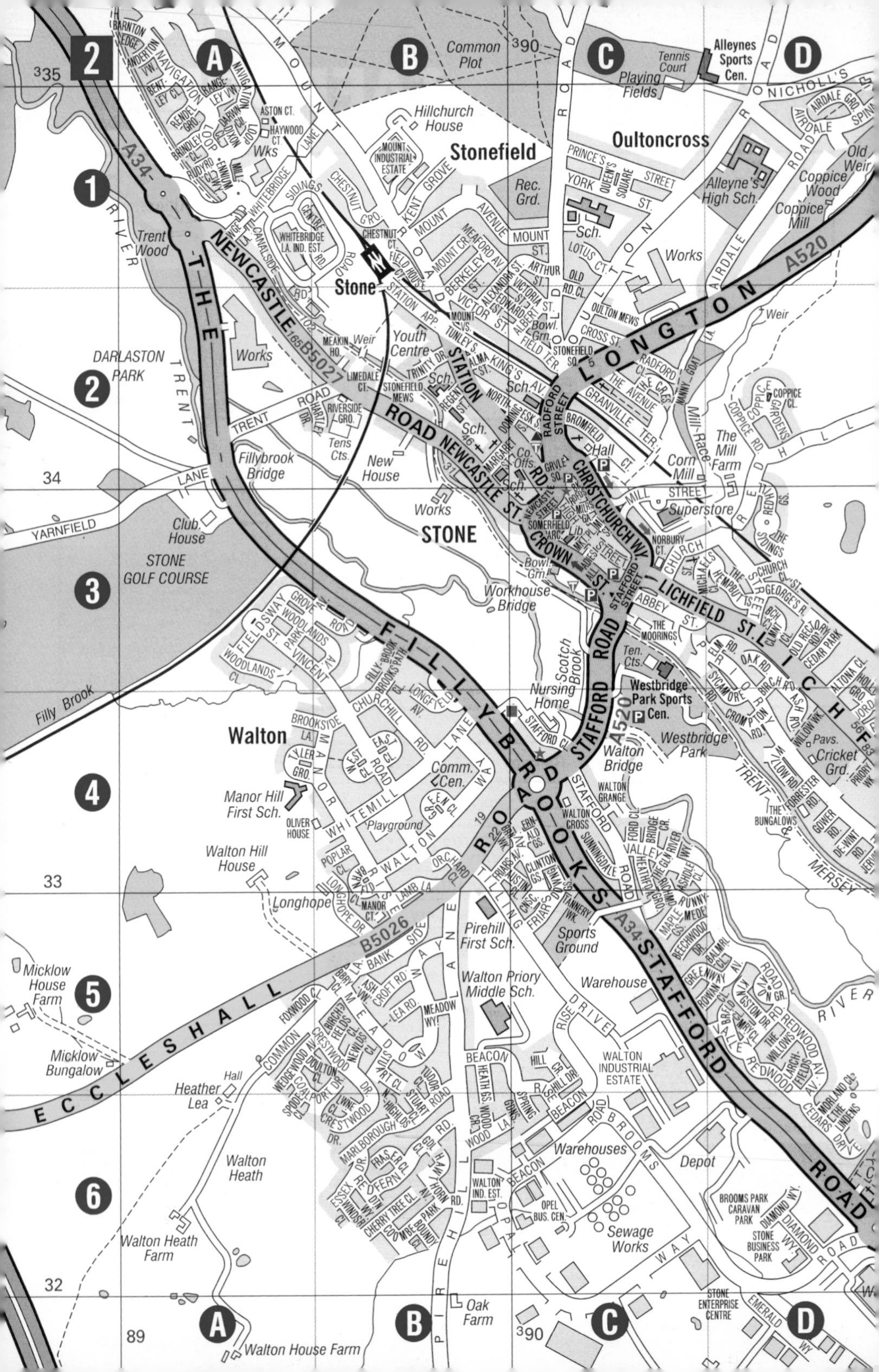
2
A
B
C
D
1
2
3
4
5
6
335
34
33
32
89
390
Common Plot
Alleynes Sports Cen.
Tennis Court
Playing Fields
Hillchurch House
Stonefield
Oultoncross
Mount Industrial Estate
Rec. Grd.
Alleyne's High Sch.
Coppice Wood
Coppice Mill
Old Weir
Trent Wood
Stone
Whitebridge La. Ind. Est.
Works
Darlaston Park
Youth Centre
Newcastle Road
B5027
Longton
A520
A34
The
Filly Brook Road
Stafford Road
Lichfield St.
Station Road
Christchurch Wy
Crown St.
Fillybrook Bridge
New House
Tens Cts.
Club House
Stone Golf Course
Yarnfield Lane
Trent Road
STONE
Superstore
Corn Mill
The Mill Farm
Mill Street
Workhouse Bridge
Scotch Brook
Nursing Home
Westbridge Park Sports Cen.
Westbridge Park
Walton Bridge
Cricket Grd.
Walton
Manor Hill First Sch.
Comm. Cen.
Playground
Walton Hill House
Longhope
Pirehill First Sch.
Sports Ground
Warehouse
Walton Priory Middle Sch.
Walton Industrial Estate
Eccleshall
B5026
Micklow House Farm
Micklow Bungalow
Heather Lea
Hall
Walton Heath
Walton Heath Farm
Warehouses
Depot
Sewage Works
Brooms Park Caravan Park
Stone Business Park
Stone Enterprise Centre
Walton Ind. Est.
Opel Bus. Cen.
Oak Farm
Walton House Farm
Filly Brook
River Trent
Pirehill Lane
Brooms Road
Emerald Wy.
Diamond Wy.

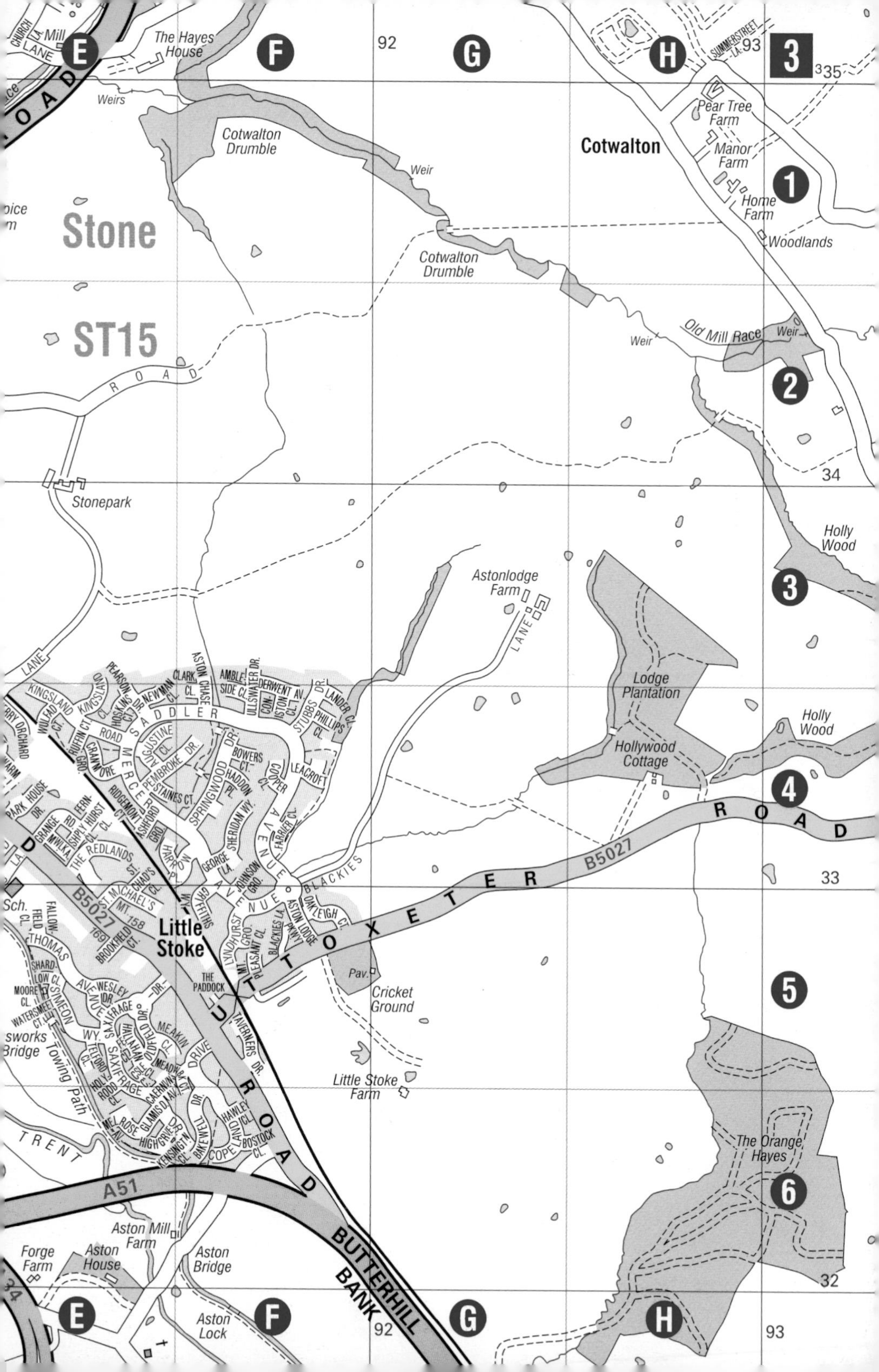
3
Stone
ST15
Cotwalton
Cotwalton Drumble
The Hayes House
Weirs
Weir
Pear Tree Farm
Manor Farm
Home Farm
Woodlands
Old Mill Race
Stonepark
Astonlodge Farm
Lodge Plantation
Hollywood Cottage
Holly Wood
UTTOXETER ROAD
B5027
Little Stoke
Cricket Ground
Pav.
Little Stoke Farm
The Orange Hayes
A51
BUTTERHILL BANK
Aston Mill Farm
Aston House
Forge Farm
Aston Bridge
Aston Lock
Towing Path
TRENT
SADDLER AVENUE
MERCER ROAD
SUMMERSTREET LA.
E
F
G
H
92
93
35
34
33
32
1
2
3
4
5
6

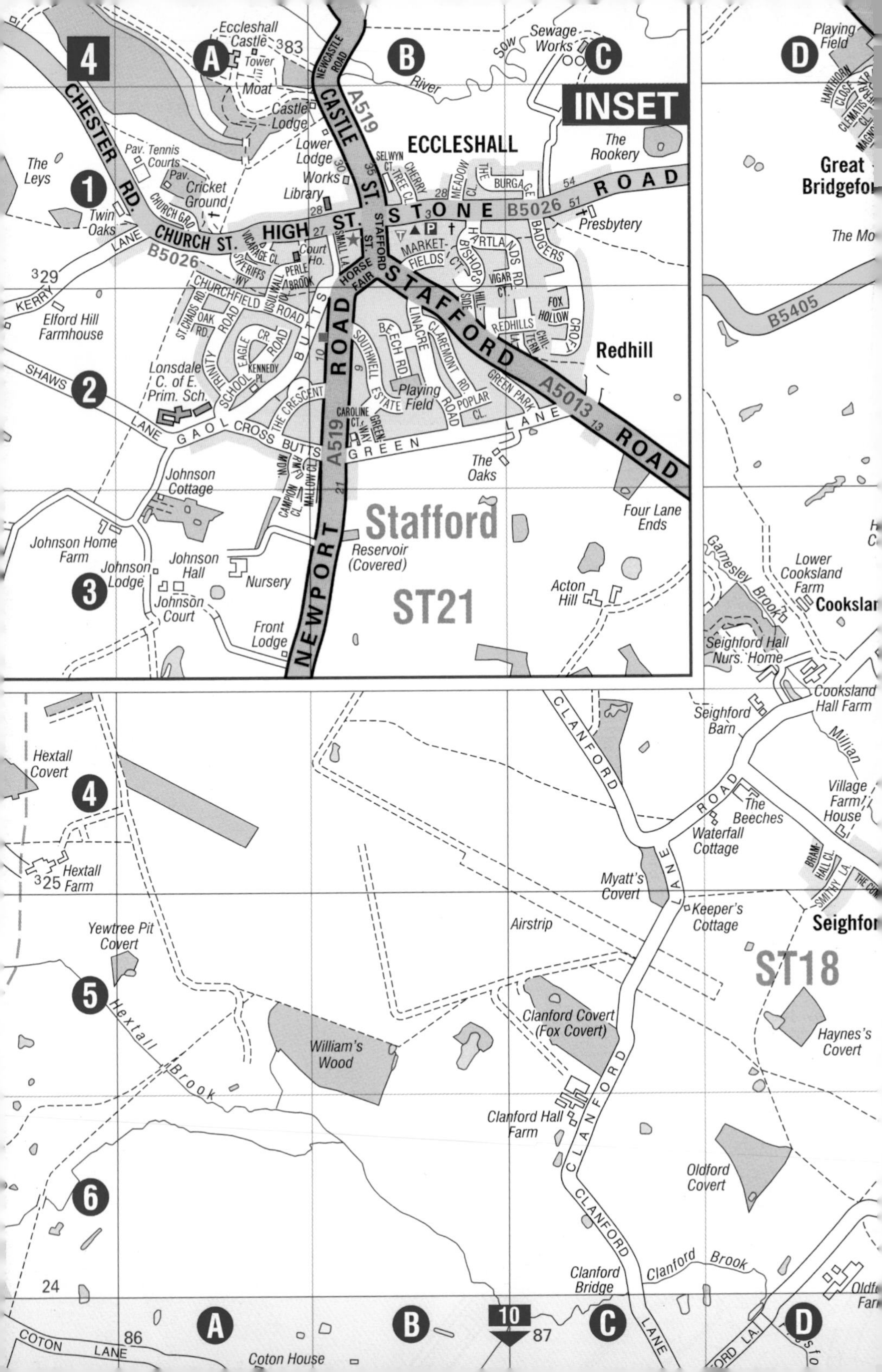

4
INSET
ECCLESHALL
Eccleshall Castle
Tower
Moat
Castle Lodge
Lower Lodge
Works
Library
Sewage Works
River Sow
The Rookery
NEWCASTLE ROAD
CASTLE ST.
A519
CHESTER RD.
STONE ROAD
B5026
HIGH ST.
CHURCH ST.
STAFFORD ST.
STAFFORD ROAD
A5013
NEWPORT ROAD
Pav. Tennis Courts
Cricket Ground
The Leys
Twin Oaks
Presbytery
Redhill
Court Ho.
Market-Fields
Horse Fair
Playing Field
Lonsdale C. of E. Prim. Sch.
GAOL BUTTS
CROSS BUTTS
GREEN LANE
SHAWS LANE
KERRY LANE
Elford Hill Farmhouse
The Oaks
Johnson Cottage
Johnson Home Farm
Johnson Lodge
Johnson Hall
Johnson Court
Nursery
Front Lodge
Stafford
Reservoir (Covered)
ST21
Four Lane Ends
Acton Hill
Great Bridgefor
B5405
Playing Field
Lower Cooksland Farm
Cooksla
Gamesley Brook
Seighford Hall Nurs. Home
Cooksland Hall Farm
Seighford Barn
Millian
Village Farm House
The Beeches
Waterfall Cottage
Myatt's Covert
Keeper's Cottage
Airstrip
Seighfor
ST18
CLANFORD ROAD
CLANFORD LANE
Hextall Covert
Hextall Farm
325
Yewtree Pit Covert
Hextall Brook
William's Wood
Clanford Covert (Fox Covert)
Haynes's Covert
Clanford Hall Farm
Oldford Covert
Clanford Bridge
Clanford Brook
COTON LANE
Coton House
24
86
87
10
A
B
C
D
1
2
3
4
5
6

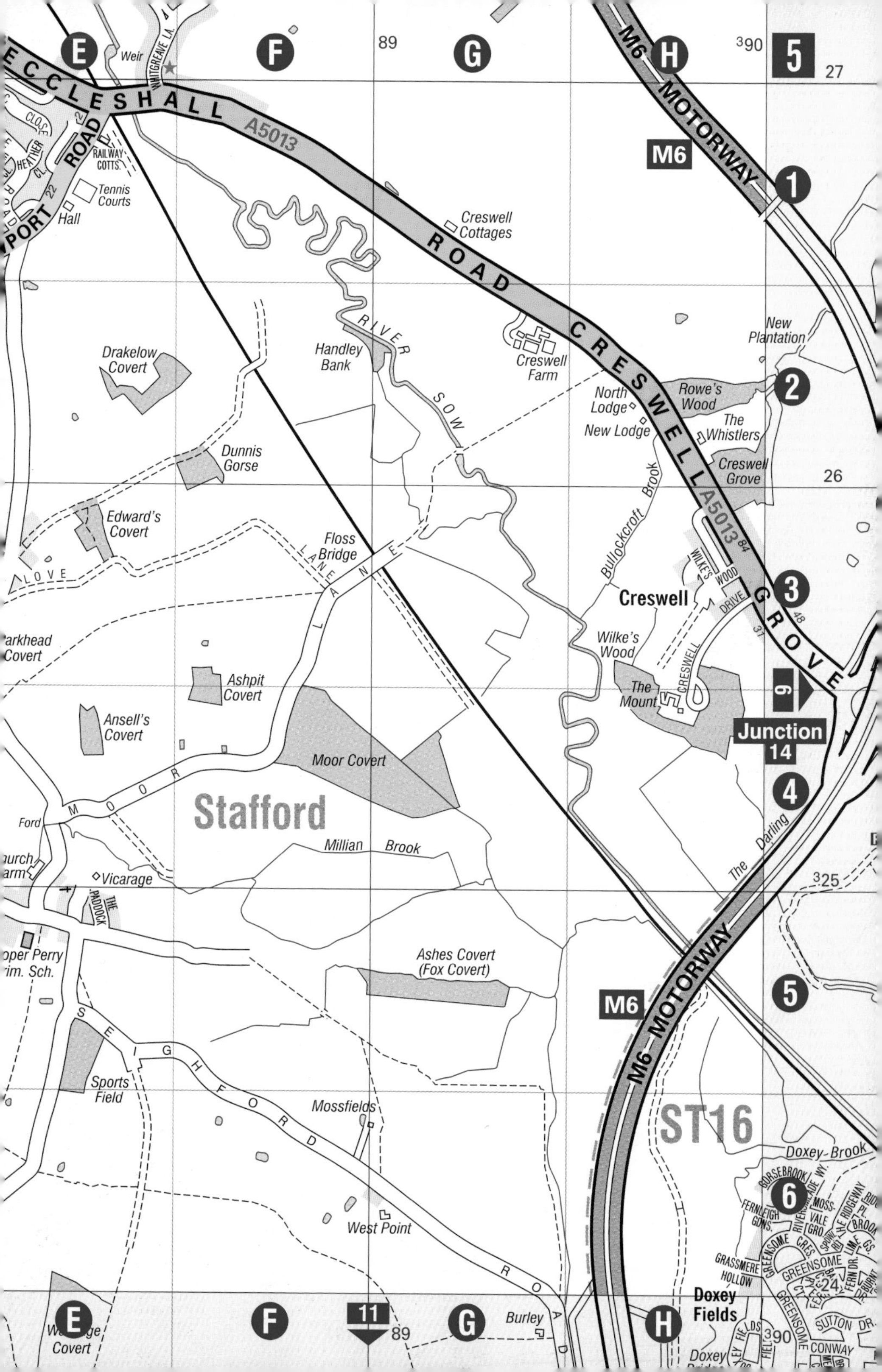

E
F
G
H
89
390
5
27
Weir
WHITGREAVE LA.
ECCLESHALL ROAD
A5013
M6 MOTORWAY
M6
1
RAILWAY COTTS.
Tennis Courts
Hall
HEATHER CL.
CLOSE
PORT ROAD
22
Creswell Cottages
ROAD
RIVER SOW
Handley Bank
CRESWELL
Creswell Farm
New Plantation
2
Drakelow Covert
North Lodge
Rowe's Wood
New Lodge
The Whistlers
Dunnis Gorse
Creswell Grove
26
Bullockcroft Brook
A5013
84
Edward's Covert
Floss Bridge
LANE
WILKE'S WOOD
3
LOVE
Creswell
DRIVE
GROVE
48
37
Parkhead Covert
Wilke's Wood
CRESWELL
Ashpit Covert
The Mount
9
Ansell's Covert
Junction 14
Moor Covert
MOOR
4
Stafford
Ford
Millian Brook
The Darling
Church Farm
Vicarage
325
THE PADDOCK
Upper Perry Prim. Sch.
Ashes Covert (Fox Covert)
M6
M6 MOTORWAY
5
SEIGHFORD ROAD
Sports Field
Mossfields
ST16
Doxey Brook
GORSEBROOK
RIVERSMEADE WY.
6
FERNLEIGH GDNS.
MOSS VALE GRO.
THE RIDGEWAY
GREENSOME CRES.
GRASSMERE HOLLOW
24
West Point
SUTTON DR.
Doxey Fields
Burley
CONWAY
11
89
390
Wanage Covert

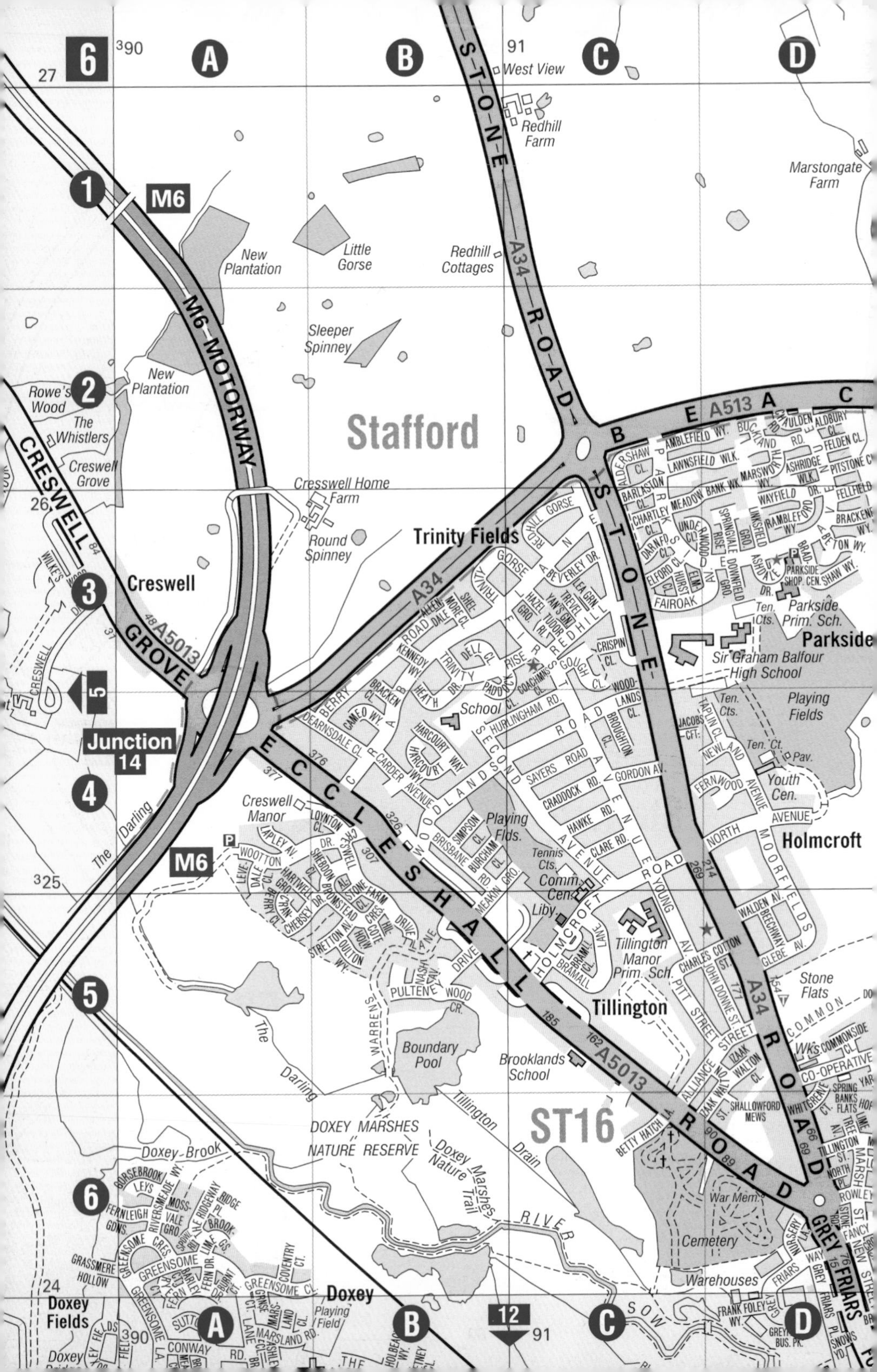

A
B
C
D
M6
M6 MOTORWAY
STONE ROAD
A34
New Plantation
Little Gorse
Redhill Cottages
West View
Redhill Farm
Marstongate Farm
Sleeper Spinney
Rowe's Wood
The Whistlers
Creswell Grove
Stafford
Cresswell Home Farm
Round Spinney
Trinity Fields
Creswell
CRESWELL GROVE
A5013
Junction 14
The Darling
Creswell Manor
A513
BEACONSIDE
Parkside
Parkside Prim. Sch.
Sir Graham Balfour High School
Playing Fields
Youth Cen.
Holmcroft
ECCLESHALL ROAD
Playing Flds.
School
Comm. Cen.
Liby.
Tillington Manor Prim. Sch.
Tillington
Stone Flats
Boundary Pool
Brooklands School
ST16
Tillington Drain
DOXEY MARSHES NATURE RESERVE
Doxey Marshes Nature Trail
Doxey Brook
RIVER SOW
War Mem.
Cemetery
Warehouses
Doxey
Doxey Fields
Playing Field
GREY FRIARS
12

Newbuildings Cottage
Newbuildings Farm
Kent's Barn Farm
Thorn Rise
ST18
R.A.F. STAFFORD Depot
R.A.F. STAFFORD
Depot
Church Hill
Lowerbridge Farm
HOPTON LANE
Mount Farm
MOUNT EDGE
B5066
SANDON ROAD
SANDON RD.
A513
Brickland Cottages
Hopton Farm
Barracks
Marston Brook
COMMON ROAD
TOLLGATE INDUSTRIAL ESTATE
BRUNEL CL.
BRINDLEY CL.
TELFORD DR.
BROOKMEAD IND. EST.
COMMON ROAD IND. EST.
Works
VERULAM RD.
VERULAM CT.
HOMESTEAD CT.
ANTOM COURT
Kingston Depot
Brook
SPODE
DOULTON RD.
WEDGWOOD RD.
RIDGEWAY CL.
TOLLGATE BUS. CEN
TENBY DRIVE
FONTHIL
CORONATION ROAD
BERTELIN ROAD
WILLIAMS CT.
THE HAYBARN
GARDENS
CHESHAM RD.
FRINTON CL.
CHARNLEY
ASTONFIELDS IND. EST.
ASTONFIELDS RD. BUS. PK.
CARVER BUS. PK.
SANDON MEWS
HOPTON ST.
OXFORD
Stafford Rangers F.C.
MARSTON RD. TRADING PK.
PETER JAMES CT.
PEEL TERRACE
VICTORIA TER.
PRINCESS PL.
Playing Fields
Beacon Farm
R.A.F. STAFFORD
BEACONSIDE
A513
PORTAL ROAD
DICKSON AVENUE
ELWORTHY CL.
PIKE CL.
TEDDER
GARROD SQUARE
NEWALL AV.
SHARMAN DR.
SALMOND ROAD
ELLINGTON AVENUE
MELBOURNE
CAIRNS DR.
CANBERRA
GLADSTONE WY.
DARWIN CL.
Kingston
Springs
MARCONI GATE
STANWAY CT.
NEWTON RD.
LISTER ROAD
DOUGLAS ROAD
WEST DOUGLAS RD.
CLEMENT CL.
BELL CL.
JUBILEE CT.
EDISON ROAD
DREIEICH CL.
FARADAY RD.
PROSPECT ROAD
Playing Field
CORPORATION ST.
SCHOOL ST.
Schs
Sch
Depot
SANDYFORD CT.
LLOYD ST.
Playgrd.
VICTORIA SQ.
CROOKED BRIDGE ROAD
H.M.P. Stafford
STREET
BLAKISTON
SMALLMAN
Rec. Grd.
SHELLEY CL.
BYRON CL.
TRENCHARD
COMM. CEN.
GRISSOM CL.
ARMSTRONG AV.
HARRIS RD.
ALDIN CL.
SALISBURY
Beaconside
St. Johns C. of E.
KNIGHT AV.
TITHE AV.
READ AV.
13
93
94
27
26
325
24
322
319
167
172
134

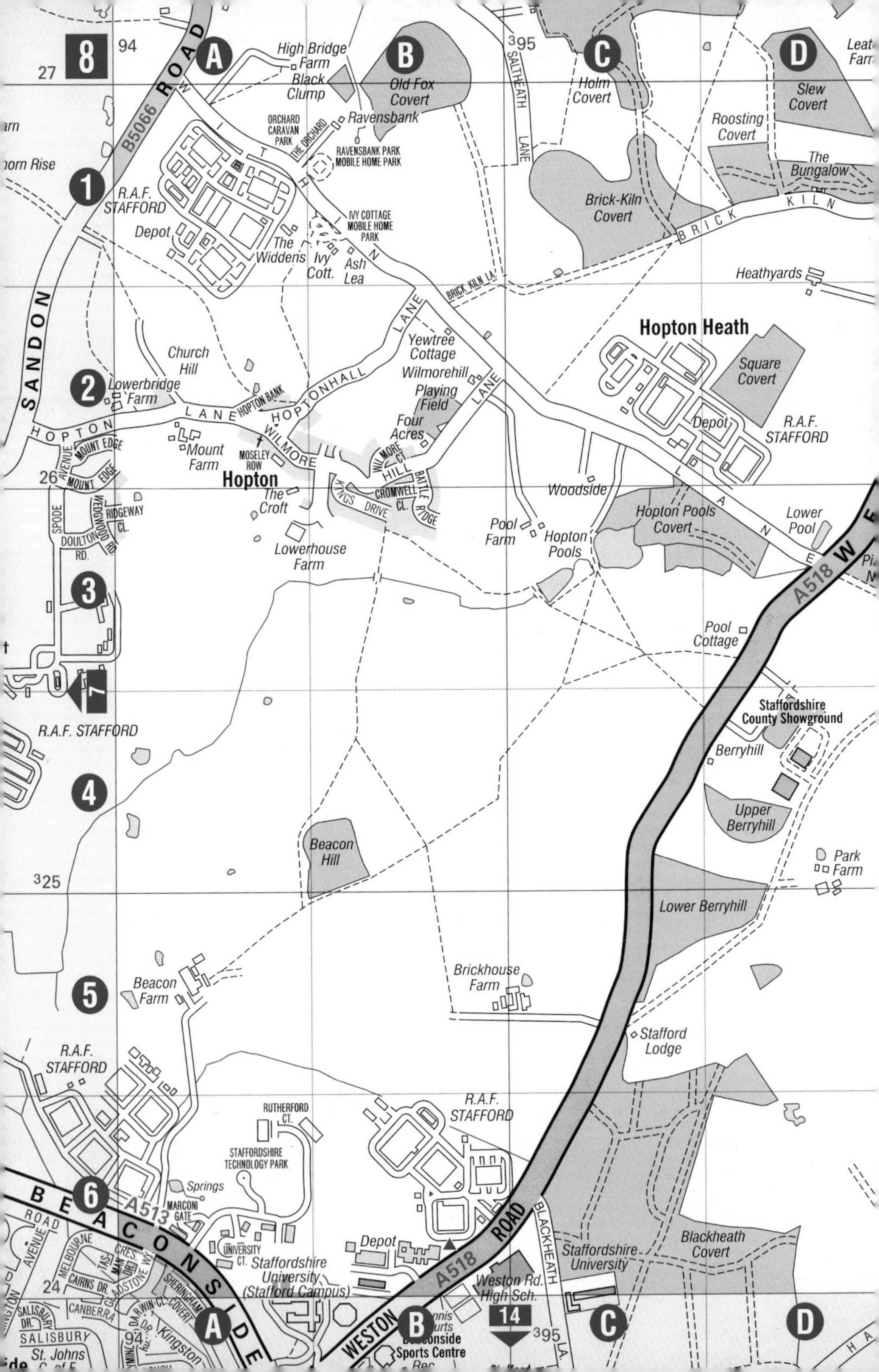
High Bridge Farm
Black Clump
Old Fox Covert
Ravensbank
ORCHARD CARAVAN PARK
THE ORCHARD
RAVENSBANK PARK MOBILE HOME PARK
SALTHEATH LANE
Holm Covert
Slew Covert
Roosting Covert
The Bungalow
Brick-Kiln Covert
BRICK KILN
B5066
SANDON ROAD
R.A.F. STAFFORD
Depot
IVY COTTAGE MOBILE HOME PARK
The Widdens
Ivy Cott.
Ash Lea
BRICK KILN LA.
Heathyards
Hopton Heath
Square Covert
Yewtree Cottage
Wilmorehill
Playing Field
Four Acres
Church Hill
Lowerbridge Farm
HOPTON BANK
HOPTONHALL LANE
HOPTON LANE
MOUNT EDGE
AVENUE
Mount Farm
MOSELEY ROW
WILMORE
Hopton
WILMORE CT.
WILMORE HILL
BATTLE RIDGE
CROMWELL CL.
KINGS DRIVE
The Croft
Lowerhouse Farm
RIDGEWAY CL.
WEDGWOOD RD.
SPODE
DOULTON RD.
Woodside
Pool Farm
Hopton Pools
Hopton Pools Covert
Lower Pool
A518
Pool Cottage
Staffordshire County Showground
Berryhill
Upper Berryhill
Park Farm
Beacon Hill
Lower Berryhill
Brickhouse Farm
Beacon Farm
Stafford Lodge
RUTHERFORD CT.
STAFFORDSHIRE TECHNOLOGY PARK
Springs
MARCONI GATE
A513
BEACONSIDE
ROAD
AVENUE
MELBOURNE
TASMAN CRES.
GLADSTONE WY.
CAIRNS DR.
CANBERRA
SALISBURY DR.
SALISBURY
SHERINGHAM COVERT
DARWIN CL.
Kingston
St. Johns
UNIVERSITY CT.
Staffordshire University (Stafford Campus)
Depot
WESTON ROAD
Weston Rd. High Sch.
BLACKHEATH LA.
Staffordshire University
Blackheath Covert
Beaconside Sports Centre
14
7
94
95
27
26
25
24

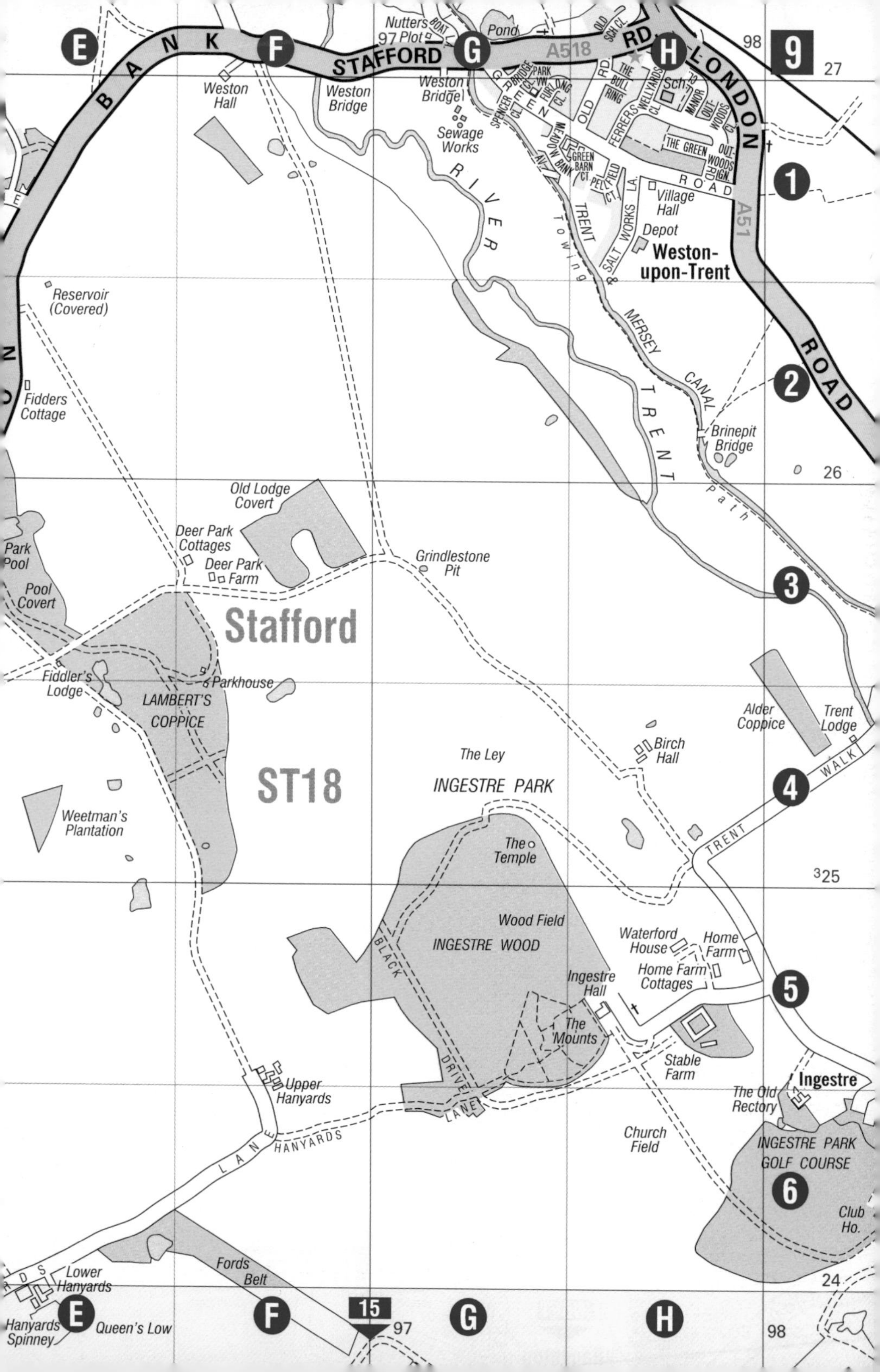
BANK
STAFFORD RD.
A518
LONDON ROAD
A51
Nutters Plot
Pond
Weston Hall
Weston Bridge
Sewage Works
RIVER TRENT
Village Hall
Depot
Weston-upon-Trent
Towing Path
TRENT & MERSEY CANAL
Brinepit Bridge
Reservoir (Covered)
Fidders Cottage
Old Lodge Covert
Deer Park Cottages
Deer Park Farm
Grindlestone Pit
Park Pool
Pool Covert
Stafford
Fiddler's Lodge
Parkhouse
LAMBERT'S COPPICE
ST18
Weetman's Plantation
The Ley
INGESTRE PARK
Birch Hall
Alder Coppice
Trent Lodge
TRENT WALK
The Temple
Wood Field
INGESTRE WOOD
BLACK DRIVE LANE
Waterford House
Home Farm
Home Farm Cottages
Ingestre Hall
The Mounts
Stable Farm
Ingestre
The Old Rectory
INGESTRE PARK GOLF COURSE
Club Ho.
Church Field
Upper Hanyards
HANYARDS LANE
Lower Hanyards
Fords Belt
Hanyards Spinney
Queen's Low
15
97
98
27
26
25
24

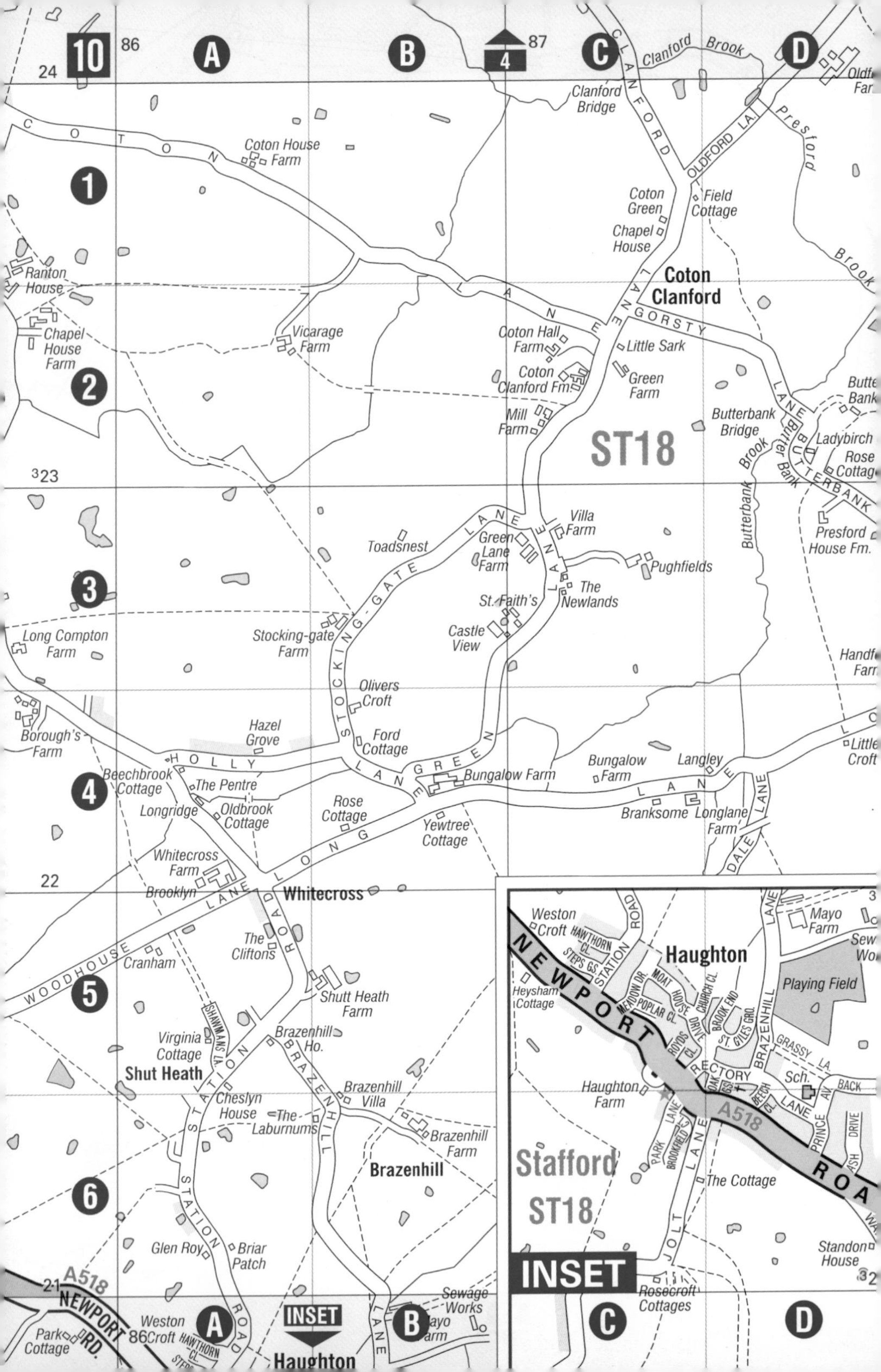

86
87
24
A
B
C
D
4
Clanford Brook
Clanford Bridge
CLANFORD
OLDFORD LA.
Presford
Oldford Farm
COTON
Coton House Farm
1
Field Cottage
Coton Green
Chapel House
Brook
Coton Clanford
Ranton House
GORSTY
LANE
Vicarage Farm
Chapel House Farm
Coton Hall Farm
Little Sark
Coton Clanford Fm.
Green Farm
2
Butterbank Bridge
Butterbank
Mill Farm
ST18
Ladybirch
BUTTERBANK
Butter Bank
Rose Cottage
323
Butterbank Brook
Villa Farm
Toadsnest
Green Lane Farm
Presford House Fm.
Pughfields
3
St. Faith's
The Newlands
Long Compton Farm
Stocking-gate Farm
STOCKING-GATE
Castle View
Handford Farm
Olivers Croft
Borough's Farm
Hazel Grove
Ford Cottage
GREEN
Little Croft
HOLLY
Bungalow Farm
Langley
Beechbrook Cottage
The Pentre
Bungalow Farm
4
Rose Cottage
Longridge
Oldbrook Cottage
Branksome
Longlane Farm
Yewtree Cottage
DALE
Whitecross Farm
LONG
22
Brooklyn
Whitecross
The Cliftons
ROAD
WOODHOUSE LANE
Cranham
Shutt Heath Farm
5
SHAWMANS LA.
Brazenhill Ho.
Virginia Cottage
BRAZENHILL
Shut Heath
Brazenhill Villa
Cheslyn House
The Laburnums
STATION
Brazenhill Farm
Brazenhill
6
STATION
Glen Roy
Briar Patch
A518
21
NEWPORT RD.
Sewage Works
Park Cottage
Weston Croft
HAWTHORN CL.
INSET
Haughton
Mayo Farm
Weston Croft
HAWTHORN CL.
STEPS GS.
STATION ROAD
Haughton
Mayo Farm
Playing Field
NEWPORT
Heysham Cottage
MEADOW DR.
MOAT HOUSE DRIVE
CHURCH CL.
POPLAR CL.
BROOK END
ST. GILES GRO.
ROYDS CL.
BRAZENHILL
GRASSY LA.
RECTORY
Sch.
BACK
Haughton Farm
OAK GS.
BEECH CL.
LANE
PRINCE AV.
A518
DRIVE
PARK LANE
BROOKFIELD CT.
Stafford
The Cottage
ST18
ROAD
ASH
JOLT LANE
Standon House
INSET
Rosecroft Cottages
C
D

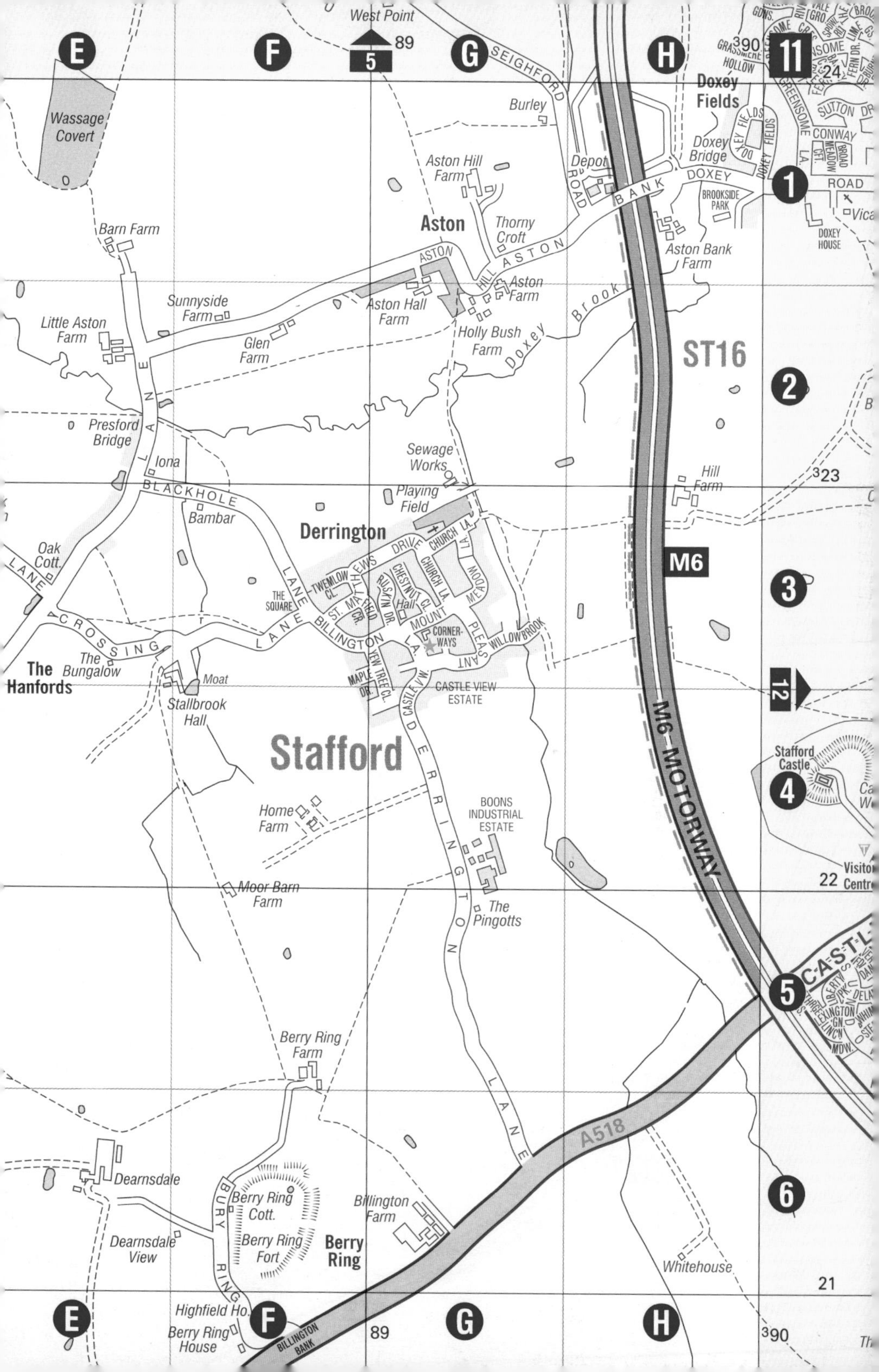

West Point
5
89
E
F
G
H
11
SEIGHFORD
390
Doxey Fields
Wassage Covert
Burley
Aston Hill Farm
Depot
ROAD
DOXEY
ROAD
BANK
Doxey Bridge
BROOKSIDE PARK
DOXEY HOUSE
Aston
Thorny Croft
Barn Farm
ASTON
HILL
Aston Bank Farm
Aston Farm
Aston Hall Farm
Sunnyside Farm
Little Aston Farm
Glen Farm
Holly Bush Farm
Doxey Brook
ST16
Presford Bridge
Iona
Sewage Works
Playing Field
Hill Farm
BLACKHOLE
Bambar
Derrington
CHURCH LA.
Oak Cott.
TWEMLOW CL.
ST. MATTHEWS DRIVE
CHESTNUT CL.
RUSKIN DR.
MEADOW
THE SQUARE
M6
CROSSING
LANE
BILLINGTON
MOUNT
PLEASANT
WILLOWBROOK
CORNER-WAYS
The Bungalow
The Hanfords
Moat
Stallbrook Hall
MAPLE DR.
YEW TREE CL.
CASTLE VIEW ESTATE
12
Stafford
DERRINGTON LANE
M6 MOTORWAY
Stafford Castle
Home Farm
BOONS INDUSTRIAL ESTATE
Moor Barn Farm
The Pingotts
Visitor Centre
22
CASTLE
Berry Ring Farm
A518
Dearnsdale
BURY RING
Berry Ring Cott.
Berry Ring Fort
Berry Ring
Billington Farm
Dearnsdale View
Whitehouse
21
Highfield Ho.
Berry Ring House
BILLINGTON BANK
390

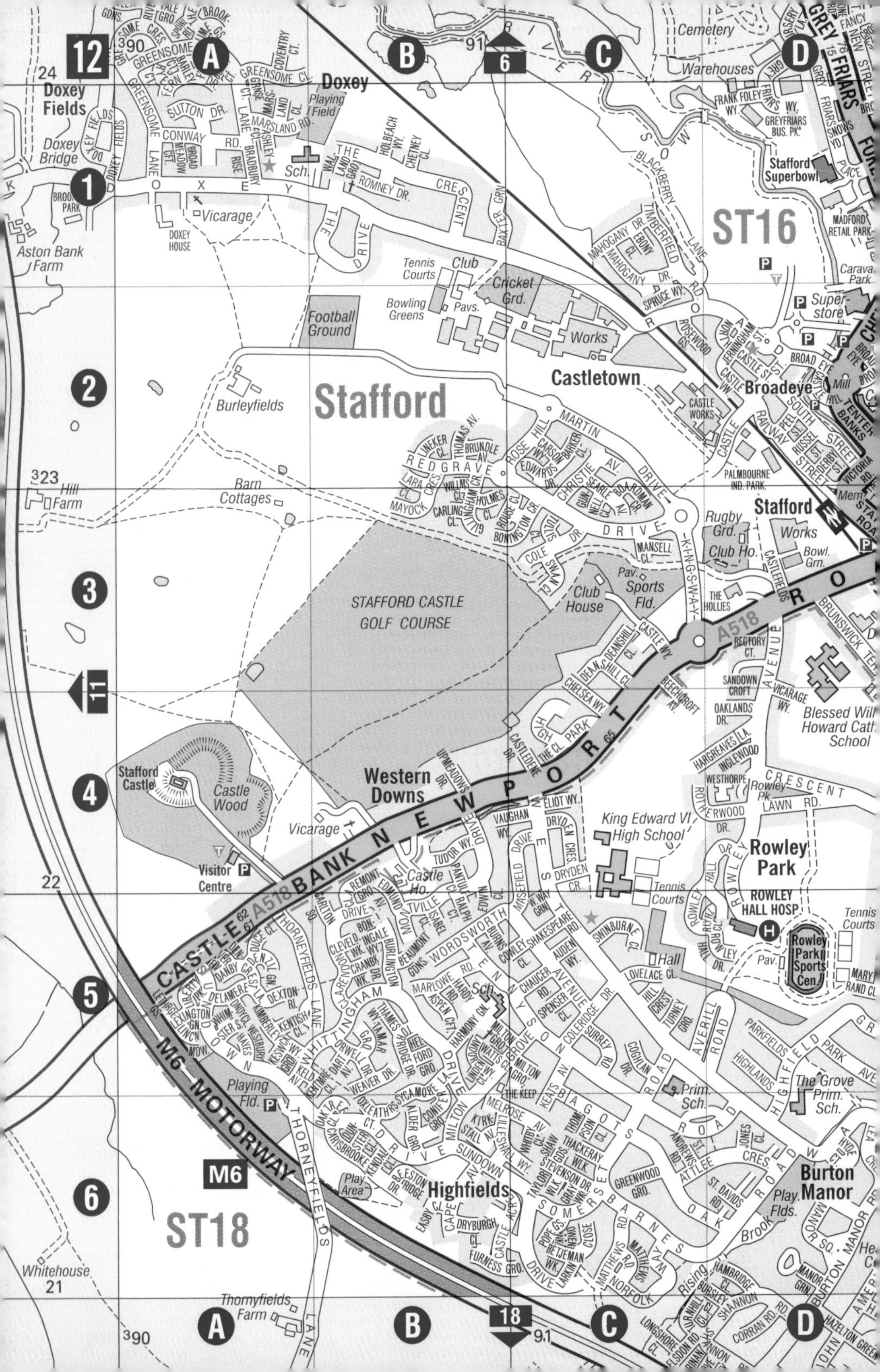

Doxey Fields
Doxey Bridge
Doxey
Playing Field
Vicarage
Doxey House
Aston Bank Farm
Hill Farm
Cemetery
Warehouses
River Sow
Greyfriars Bus. Pk.
Stafford Superbowl
ST16
Madford Retail Park
Superstore
Tennis Courts
Club
Cricket Grd.
Bowling Greens
Pavs.
Football Ground
Works
Castletown
Broadeye
Castle Works
Palmbourne Ind. Park.
Stafford
Stafford
Burleyfields
Barn Cottages
Rugby Grd.
Club Ho.
Bowl. Grn.
Sports Fld.
Club House
Stafford Castle Golf Course
The Hollies
Blessed William Howard Catholic School
Stafford Castle
Castle Wood
Western Downs
Vicarage
Visitor Centre
King Edward VI High School
Rowley Park
Rowley Hall Hosp
Rowley Park Sports Cen.
Tennis Courts
Castle Ho.
Hall
Newport Road
Castle Bank
A518
M6 Motorway
M6
Playing Fld.
Play Area
Highfields
ST18
Whitehouse
Thornyfields Farm
The Grove Prim. Sch.
Prim. Sch.
Burton Manor
Play. Flds.
Sch.
6
11
18
A B C D
1 2 3 4 5 6

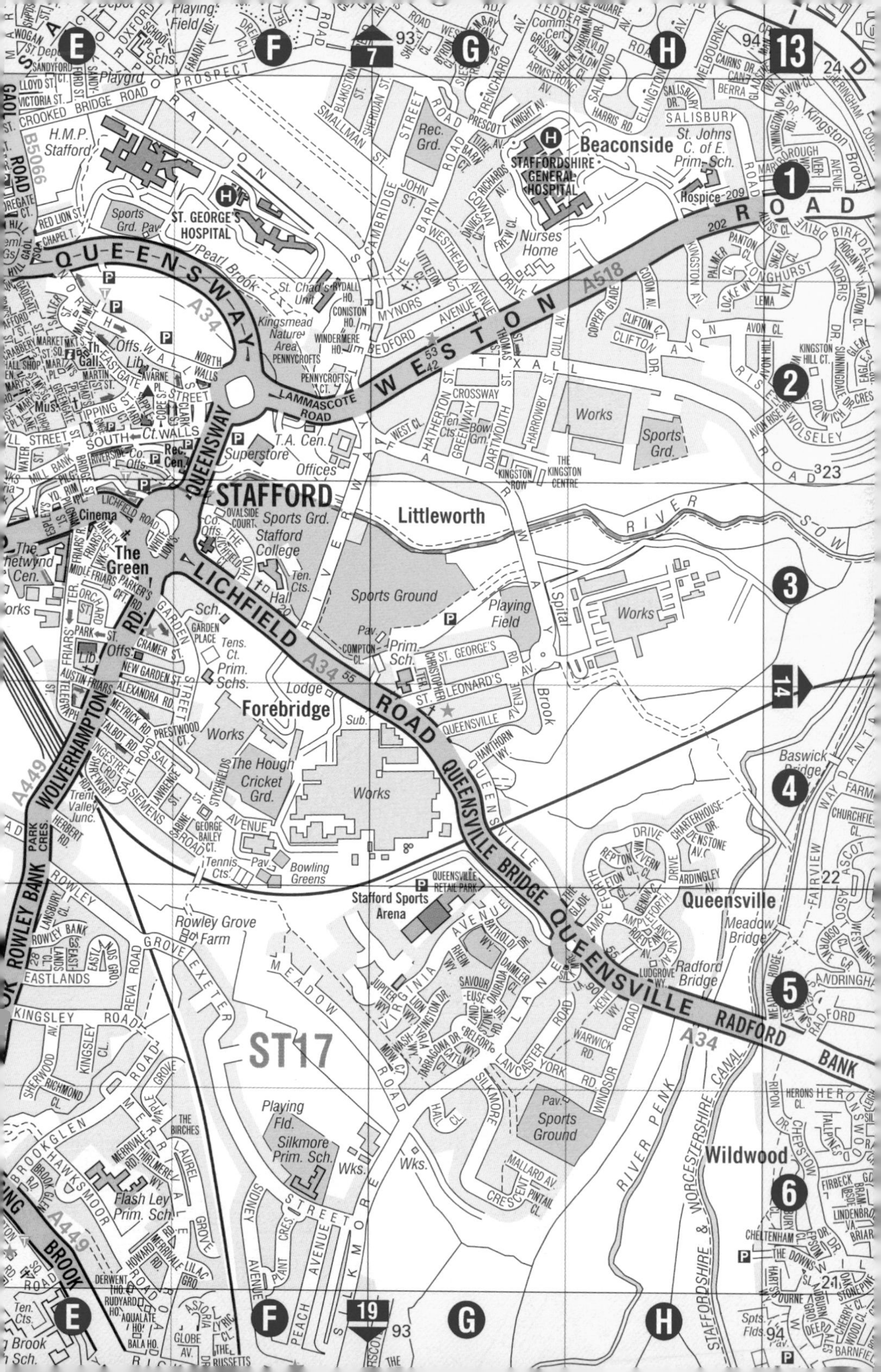
E
F
G
H
7
93
94
1
2
3
4
5
6
14
19
24
23
22
21
QUEENSWAY
A34
WESTON ROAD
A518
LICHFIELD ROAD
QUEENSVILLE BRIDGE
QUEENSVILLE
RADFORD BANK
WOLVERHAMPTON RD.
ROWLEY BANK
A449
B5066
GAOL ROAD
CROOKED BRIDGE ROAD
PROSPECT
H.M.P. Stafford
Playgrd
Playing Field
Schs.
ST. GEORGE'S HOSPITAL
Sports Grd. Pav.
Pearl Brook
Kingsmead Nature Area
St. Chad's Unit
RYDALL HO.
CONISTON HO.
WINDERMERE HO.
PENNYCROFTS
PENNYCROFTS CT.
LAMMASCOTE ROAD
Rec. Grd.
STAFFORDSHIRE GENERAL HOSPITAL
Beaconside
St. Johns C. of E. Prim. Sch.
Hospice
Nurses Home
SALISBURY
MARLBOROUGH AVENUE
BIRKDALE
LONGHURST
CLIFTON DR.
AVON RISE
WOLSELEY ROAD
KINGSTON HILL CT.
Works
Sports Grd.
THE KINGSTON CENTRE
KINGSTON ROW
TIXALL
CROSSWAY
Bowl. Grn.
Ten. Cts.
T.A. Cen.
Superstore
Offices
STAFFORD
OVALSIDE COURT
Sports Grd.
Stafford College
Littleworth
RIVER SOW
Sports Ground
Playing Field
Spital
Works
Prim. Sch.
ST. GEORGE'S RD.
ST. LEONARD'S AV.
QUEENSVILLE AVENUE
HAWTHORN WY.
Brook
Baswick Bridge
Mus.
Lib.
Offs.
Cinema
The Chetwynd Cen.
The Green
Forebridge
Tens. Ct.
Prim. Schs.
Works
The Hough Cricket Grd.
Works
Lodge
Sub.
Bowling Greens
Tennis Cts.
Pav.
Trent Valley Junc.
QUEENSVILLE RETAIL PARK
Stafford Sports Arena
Rowley Grove Farm
GROVE
EXETER
MEADOW ROAD
ST17
VIRGINIA AVENUE
Queensville
Meadow Bridge
Radford Bridge
Wildwood
RIVER PENK
STAFFORDSHIRE & WORCESTERSHIRE CANAL
EASTLANDS
KINGSLEY ROAD
MERRIVALE
Flash Ley Prim. Sch.
BROOKGLEN
HAWKSMOOR
Playing Fld.
Silkmore Prim. Sch.
Wks.
SILKMORE LANE
SIDNEY AVENUE
PEACH AVENUE
LANCASTER ROAD
WINDSOR ROAD
Sports Ground
MALLARD AV.
CRESCENT
Spts. Flds.
CHELTENHAM
THE DOWNS
FIRBECK
CHEPSTOW
HERONS CL.
BROOK
A449
Ten. Cts.
Brook Sch.
GLOBE AV.
THE RUSSETTS

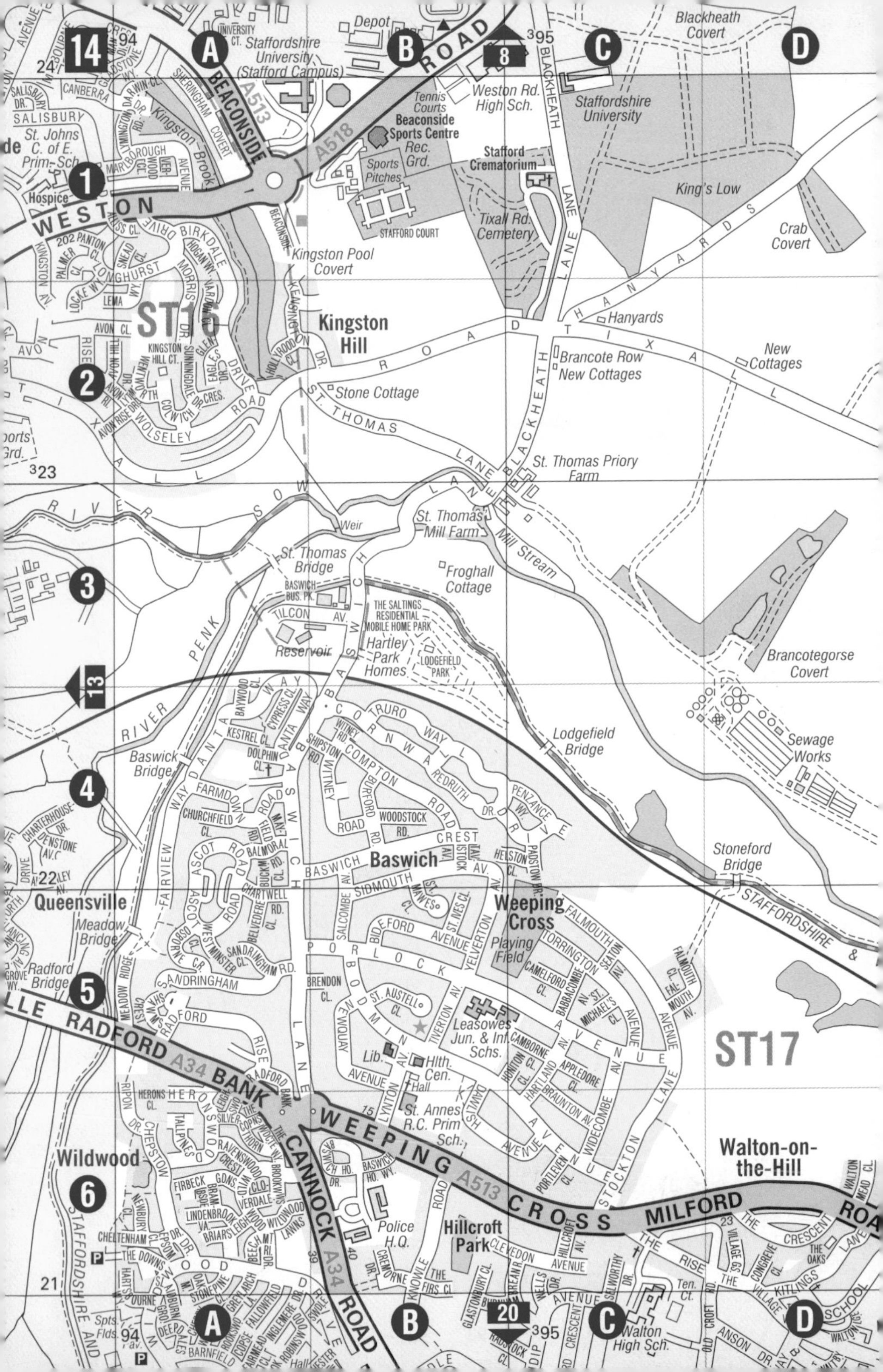

14
A
B
C
D
1
2
3
4
5
6
Staffordshire University (Stafford Campus)
Depot
Beaconside Sports Centre
Rec. Grd.
Sports Pitches
Tennis Courts
Weston Rd. High Sch.
Blackheath Covert
Staffordshire University
Stafford Crematorium
Tixall Rd. Cemetery
King's Low
Crab Covert
Stafford Court
Kingston Pool Covert
Kingston Hill
Kingston Hill Ct.
St. Johns C. of E. Prim. Sch.
Hospice
ST16
ST17
Hanyards
Brancote Row New Cottages
New Cottages
Stone Cottage
St. Thomas Priory Farm
St. Thomas' Mill Farm
Froghall Cottage
Mill Stream
Weir
St. Thomas Bridge
River Sow
River Penk
Baswich Bus. Pk.
The Saltings Residential Mobile Home Park
Hartley Park Homes
Lodgefield Park
Reservoir
Brancotegorse Covert
Sewage Works
Lodgefield Bridge
Stoneford Bridge
Staffordshire &
Baswick Bridge
Baswich
Weeping Cross
Playing Field
Leasowes Jun. & Inf. Schs.
Lib.
Hlth. Cen.
Hall
St. Annes R.C. Prim Sch.
Queensville
Meadow Bridge
Radford Bridge
Wildwood
Police H.Q.
Hillcroft Park
Walton-on-the-Hill
Walton High Sch.
Spts. Flds.
Beaconside
A513
A518
Road
Weston
Tixall Road
Blackheath Lane
Hanyards
Kingston Avenue
Birkdale Drive
Wolseley Road
St. Thomas Lane
Baswich Lane
Cornwall Drive
Compton Road
Danta Way
Farmdown Road
Fairview Way
Ascot Road
Sandringham Rd.
Porlock Avenue
Bodmin Avenue
Bideford Avenue
Sidmouth Avenue
Torrington Avenue
Falmouth Avenue
Stockton Lane
Radford Bank
A34
Weeping Cross
Milford Road
Cannock Road
Wildwood Drive
Clevedon Avenue
The Rise
The Crescent
Meadow Ridge
Staffordshire and
Heronsbrook
13
8
20
394
395
323
322
321

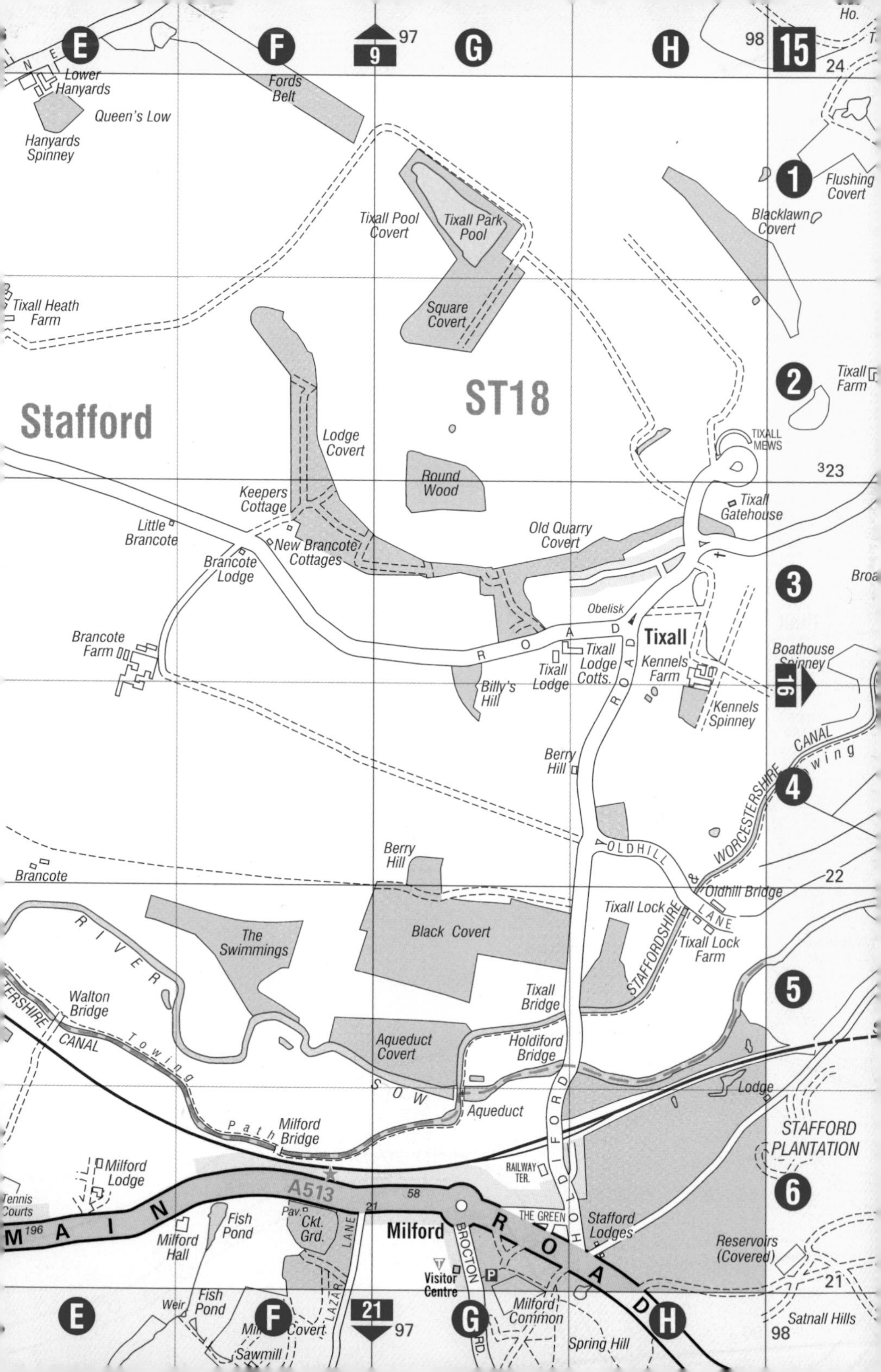
15
Lower Hanyards
Queen's Low
Hanyards Spinney
Fords Belt
Tixall Pool Covert
Tixall Park Pool
Square Covert
Flushing Covert
Blacklawn Covert
Tixall Heath Farm
Tixall Farm
ST18
Stafford
Lodge Covert
TIXALL MEWS
Round Wood
Keepers Cottage
Tixall Gatehouse
Little Brancote
New Brancote Cottages
Old Quarry Covert
Brancote Lodge
Obelisk
Tixall
Brancote Farm
ROAD
Tixall Lodge Cotts.
Tixall Lodge
Boathouse Spinney
Kennels Farm
Billy's Hill
Kennels Spinney
16
WORCESTERSHIRE CANAL
Towing
Berry Hill
OLDHILL LANE
Brancote
Oldhill Bridge
Tixall Lock
Black Covert
Tixall Lock Farm
RIVER
The Swimmings
STAFFORDSHIRE
Walton Bridge
Tixall Bridge
Aqueduct Covert
Holdiford Bridge
SOW
Lodge
Aqueduct
Path
Milford Bridge
STAFFORD PLANTATION
Milford Lodge
RAILWAY TER.
A513
MAIN ROAD
Tennis Courts
Fish Pond
Pav.
Ckt. Grd.
LAZAR LANE
Milford
BROCTON RD.
THE GREEN
HOLDIFORD
Stafford Lodges
Milford Hall
Reservoirs (Covered)
Visitor Centre
Weir
Fish Pond
Milford Common
Satnall Hills
21
Spring Hill
Sawmill
Covert
E F G H
1 2 3 4 5 6
97 98 24 323 22 21 196 58 9

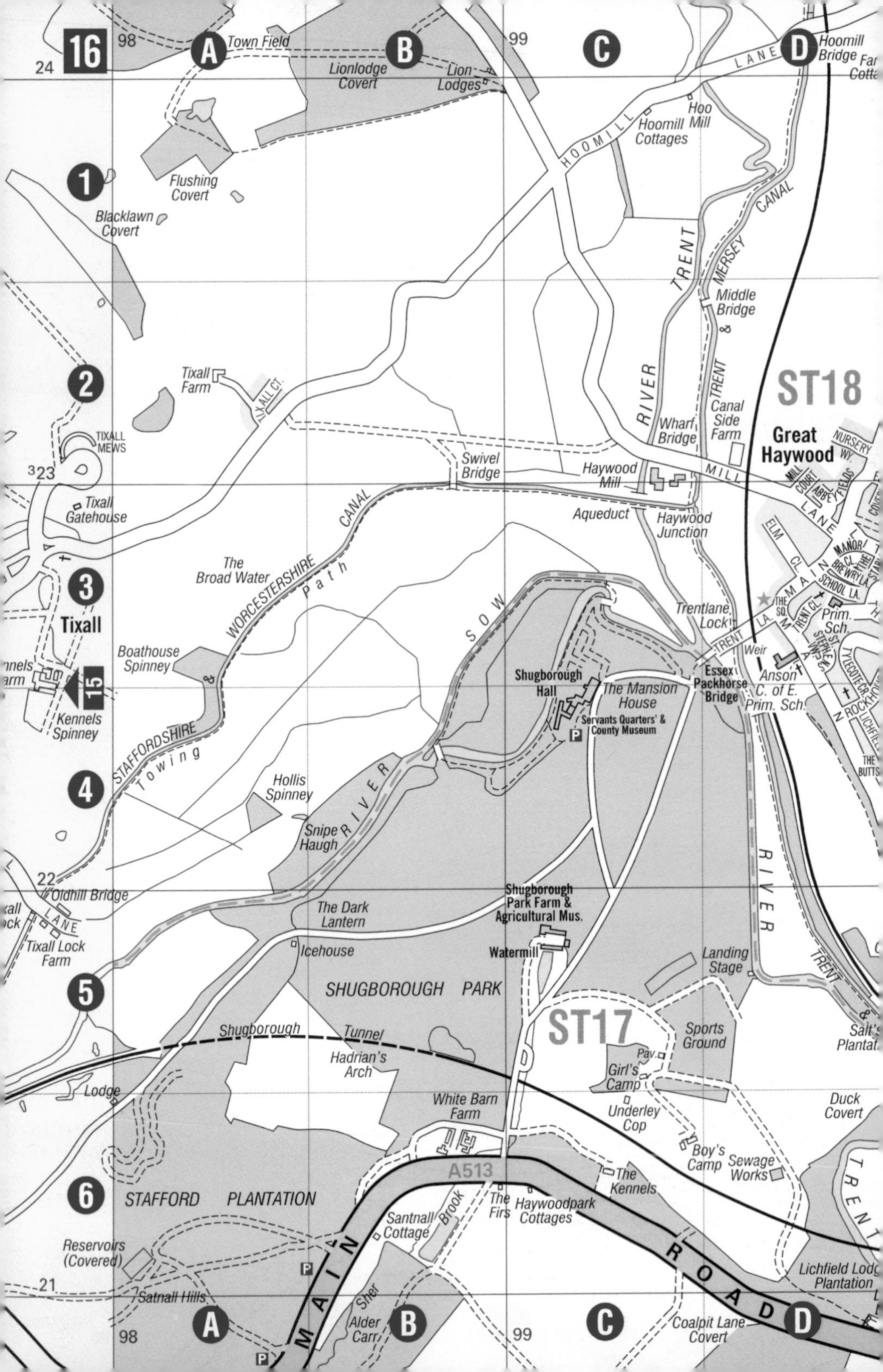
Town Field
Lionlodge Covert
Lion Lodges
Hoomill Lane
Hoomill Bridge
Hoomill Cottages
Hoo Mill
Flushing Covert
Blacklawn Covert
Trent & Mersey Canal
River Trent
Middle Bridge
ST18
Tixall Farm
Tixall Ct.
Tixall Mews
Canal Side Farm
Wharf Bridge
Great Haywood
Tixall Gatehouse
Swivel Bridge
Haywood Mill
Mill Lane
Aqueduct
Haywood Junction
Staffordshire & Worcestershire Canal
Towing Path
The Broad Water
Tixall
River Sow
Trentlane Lock
Trent La.
Weir
Boathouse Spinney
Shugborough Hall
The Mansion House
Servants Quarters' & County Museum
Essex Packhorse Bridge
Anson C. of E. Prim. Sch.
Kennels Spinney
15
Hollis Spinney
Snipe Haugh
Oldhill Bridge
Tixall Lock Farm
The Dark Lantern
Shugborough Park Farm & Agricultural Mus.
Watermill
Icehouse
Landing Stage
Shugborough Park
Shugborough Tunnel
ST17
Sports Ground
Hadrian's Arch
Pav.
Girl's Camp
Lodge
White Barn Farm
Underley Cop
Duck Covert
Boy's Camp
Sewage Works
A513
The Kennels
The Firs
Haywoodpark Cottages
Stafford Plantation
Santnall Cottage
Brook
Main Road
Reservoirs (Covered)
Satnall Hills
Sher
Alder Carr
Coalpit Lane Covert
Lichfield Lodge Plantation
Salt's Plantation

INSET
Stafford
ST18
Tolldish
TOLLDISH LANE
FARLEY
Hixon
HIXON AIRFIELD ESTATE
HIXON AIRFIELD INDUSTRIAL ESTATE
NEW ROAD ESTATE
Heath Farm
Hixon Heath
HIXON IND. EST.
Ashe House
Mount Farm
Green Fields
STOWE LANE
CHURCH RD.
BACK LA.
FEATHERBED LA.
SMITHY LA.
HIGH ST.
NEW ROAD
Yew Tree Farm
Grange Farm
EGG LANE
Little Covert
Tithebarn Covert
Jewstrup Covert
OLDFIELDS LA.
Little Tixall
TIXALL LANE
Oaklands Farm
Coley
COLEY LANE
Higher Coley Farm
Far Coley Farm
Stafford
Kilnhurst Covert
Playing Field
ANSON'S ROW
PINFOLD TER.
Little Haywood
SHUGBOROUGH TER.
THE BUTTS
BACK LANE
COLEY GRO.
HIGHFIELD DR.
KINGSCROFT
BILLINGTON AV.
PENN CFT.
HILLSIDE
MAIN ROAD
KINGFISHER DRIVE
Cross Heads
A51
St. Mary's Convent Fm.
St. Mary's Abbey
Navigation Farm
CANAL
Meadowlane Bridge
MEADOW LANE
Colwich Prim. Sch.
RAILWAY COTTS.
STATION RD.
THE MOORINGS
Overdale
Colwich
Colwich Lock
Colwich Bridge
Church Farm
The Gables
Bishton Lane Farm
BISHTON LA.
E F G H
1 2 3 4 5 6
01 02 400 326 323 22 21

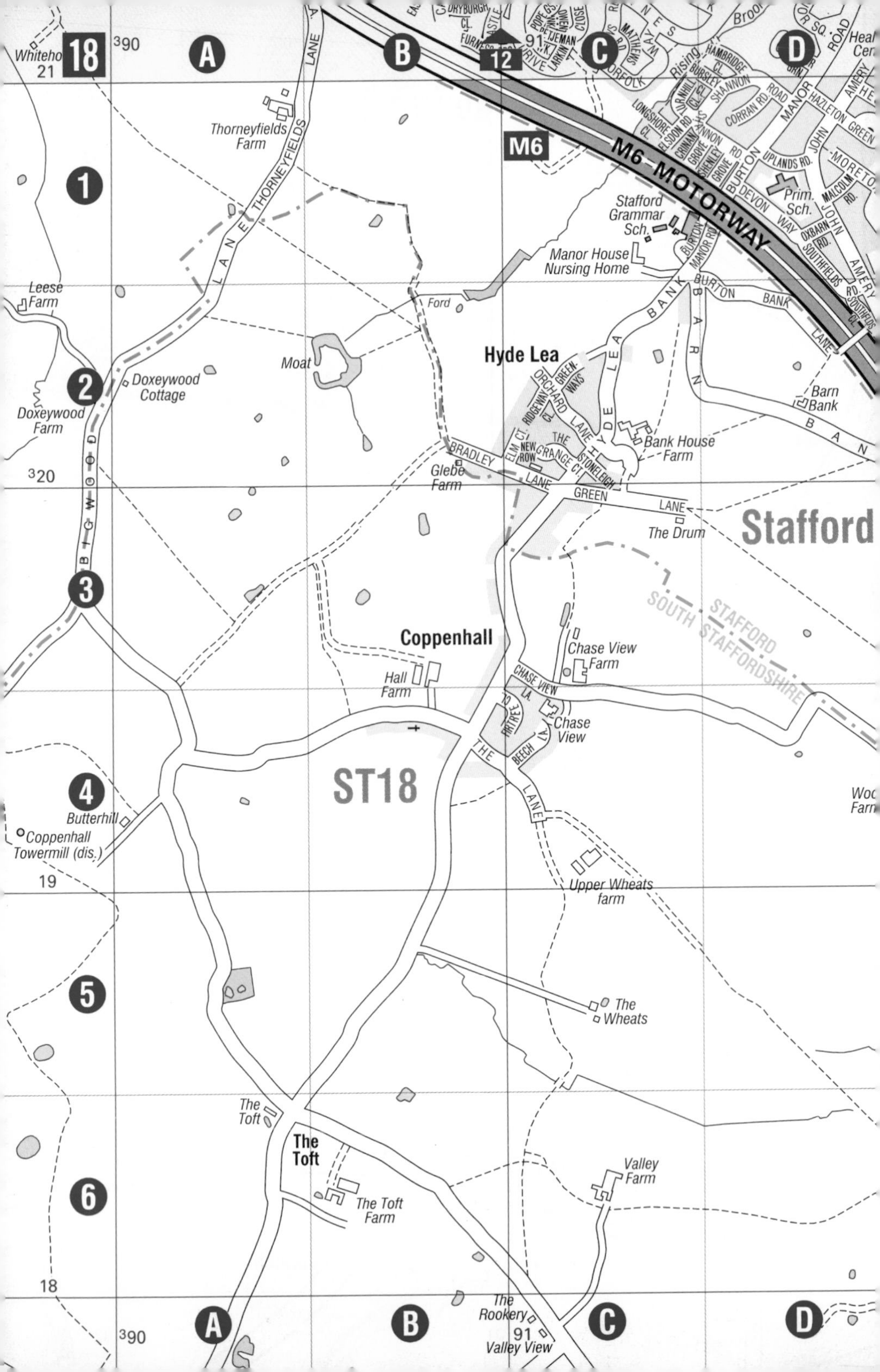

18
Whiteho
21
390
A
B
C
D
12
91
M6
M6 MOTORWAY
1
2
3
4
5
6
Thorneyfields Farm
THORNEYFIELDS LANE
Leese Farm
Doxeywood Cottage
Doxeywood Farm
BIGWOOD
320
Moat
Ford
Stafford Grammar Sch.
Manor House Nursing Home
Hyde Lea
HYDE LEA BANK
BURTON BANK
BURTON BANK LANE
BARN BANK
Barn Bank
Bank House Farm
ORCHARD LANE
GREENWAYS
RIDGEWAY CL.
ELM CT.
NEW ROW
THE GRANGE CT.
STONELEIGH
BRADLEY LANE
GREEN LANE
Glebe Farm
The Drum
Stafford
STAFFORD
SOUTH STAFFORDSHIRE
Coppenhall
Chase View Farm
CHASE VIEW LA.
Hall Farm
Chase View
FIRTREE CL.
BEECH LA.
THE LANE
ST18
Butterhill
Coppenhall Towermill (dis.)
19
Upper Wheats farm
The Wheats
Woo Farm
The Toft
Valley Farm
The Toft Farm
18
The Rookery
Valley View
Prim. Sch.
MANOR ROAD
DEVON WAY
UPLANDS RD.
CORRAN RD.
MALCOLM RD.
OXBARN RD.
SOUTHFIELDS
AMERY
HAZLETON GREEN
Rising Brook

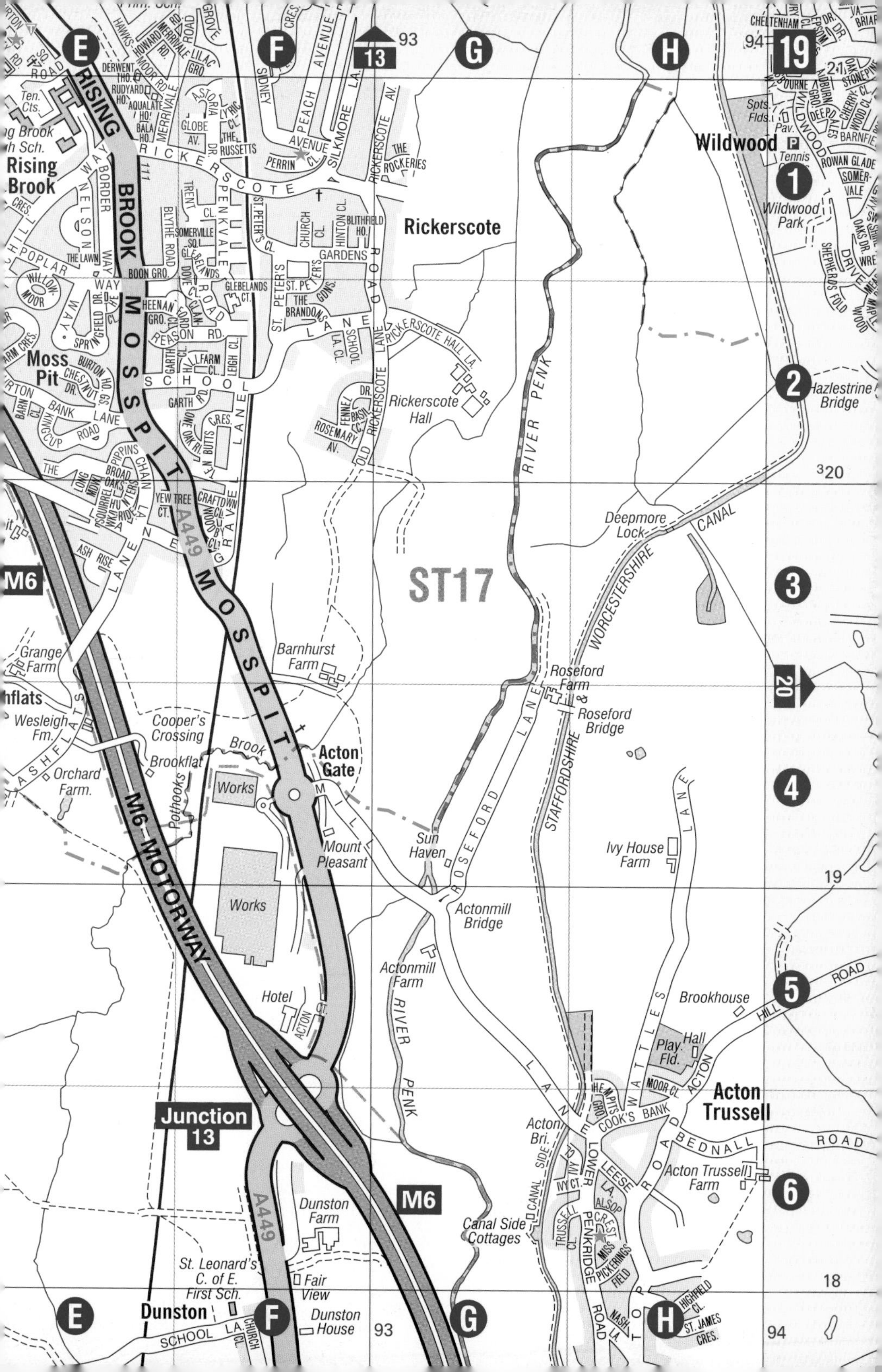

19
E
F
G
H
13
93
94
Wildwood
Wildwood Park
Hazlestrine Bridge
Rising Brook
Rickerscote
Rickerscote Hall
Moss Pit
ST17
RIVER PENK
Deepmore Lock
STAFFORDSHIRE & WORCESTERSHIRE CANAL
Barnhurst Farm
Roseford Farm
Roseford Bridge
ROSEFORD LANE
Grange Farm
Wesleigh Fm.
Cooper's Crossing
Brookflat
Orchard Farm.
Works
Acton Gate
Mount Pleasant
Sun Haven
Actonmill Bridge
Actonmill Farm
Ivy House Farm
Brookhouse
Hotel
Play. Fld.
Hall
Acton Trussell
Acton Trussell Farm
Acton Bri.
Canal Side Cottages
Dunston Farm
St. Leonard's C. of E. First Sch.
Dunston
Fair View
Dunston House
Junction 13
M6
M6 MOTORWAY
A449
MOSS PIT
RISING BROOK
RICKERSCOTE ROAD
SCHOOL LANE
BEDNALL ROAD
HILL ROAD
WATTLES LANE
COOK'S BANK
LOWER PENKRIDGE ROAD
CANAL SIDE
SCHOOL LA.
CHURCH CL.
1
2
3
4
5
6
20
320
19
18

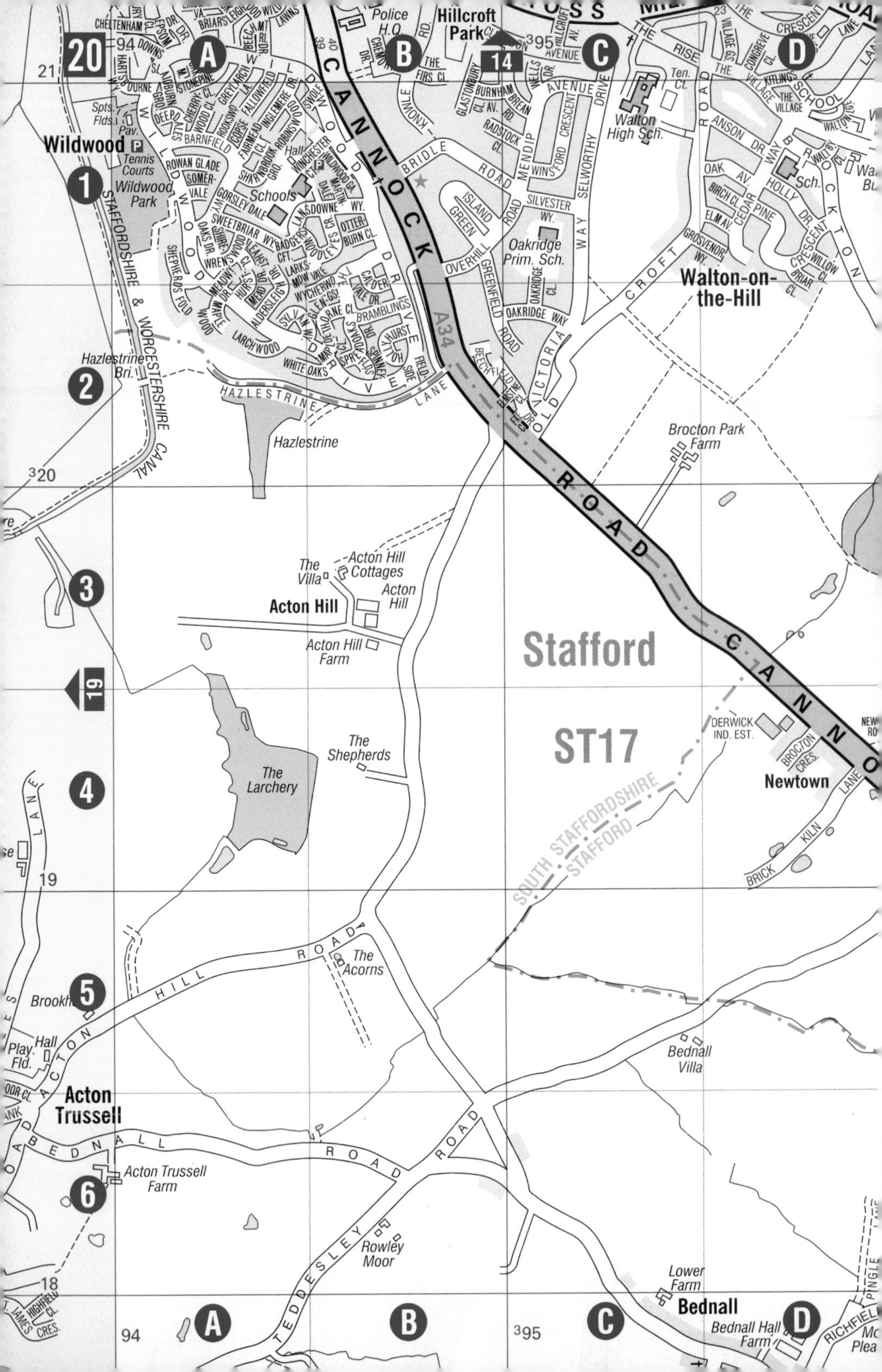

20
14
19
A
B
C
D
1
2
3
4
5
6
94
395
21
20
19
18
Police H.Q.
Hillcroft Park
Wildwood
Tennis Courts
Wildwood Park
Spts. Flds.
Pav.
Schools
Hall
Walton High Sch.
Sch.
Oakridge Prim. Sch.
Walton-on-the-Hill
CANNOCK ROAD
A34
STAFFORDSHIRE & WORCESTERSHIRE CANAL
Hazlestrine Bri.
HAZLESTRINE LANE
Hazlestrine
Brocton Park Farm
The Villa
Acton Hill Cottages
Acton Hill
Acton Hill Farm
Stafford
ST17
The Larchery
The Shepherds
DERWICK IND. EST.
BROCTON CRES.
Newtown
BRICK KILN LANE
SOUTH STAFFORDSHIRE
STAFFORD
ACTON HILL ROAD
The Acorns
Play. Fld.
Hall
Acton Trussell
BEDNALL ROAD
Acton Trussell Farm
TEDDESLEY ROAD
Rowley Moor
Bednall Villa
Lower Farm
Bednall
Bednall Hall Farm
PINGLE
RICHFIELD
HIGHFIELD CL.
ST. JAMES CRES.
BRIDLE ROAD
MENDIP AVENUE
SELWORTHY DRIVE
CRESCENT
WINSFORD
SILVESTER WY.
ISLAND GREEN
OVERHILL
GREENFIELD ROAD
OAKRIDGE WAY
OAKRIDGE CL.
VICTORIA
OLD
CROFT
GROSVENOR WY.
THE RISE
ANSON DR.
OAK AV.
BIRCH CL.
ELM AV.
CEDAR
PINE
HOLLY DR.
CRESCENT
WILLOW
BRIAR CL.
BROCKTON
SCHOOL
KITLINGS
THE VILLAGE
CONGREVE CL.
VILLAGE GS.
AVENUE
WELLS DR.
GLASTONBURY CL.
BURNHAM AV.
BREAN RD.
RADSTOCK CL.
KNOWLE RD.
THE FIRS CL.
CREMORNE DR.
WILDWOOD DRIVE
SWOLE
WINCHESTER CT.
LANSDOWNE WY.
OTTERBURN CL.
BADGERS CFT.
LARKS-MDW
VALE
WYCHERWD.
CALDER
VALE DR.
BRAMBLINGS
THORNE CL.
SPINNEY
FIELD-SIDE
WHITE OAKS
LARCHWOOD
SHEPHERDS FOLD
ROWAN GLADE
SOMERVILLE
GORSLEY DALE
SWEETBRIAR WY.
OAKS DR.
WRENSWOOD
ALDERSLEIGH DR.
BARNFIELD
FALLOWFIELD
INGLEMERE DR.
ROBINSWOOD
CHERRY CL.
STONEPINE
AUBURN GRO.
CHELTENHAM
EPSOM
DOWNS
BRIARS
LAWNS
BEECHFIELD

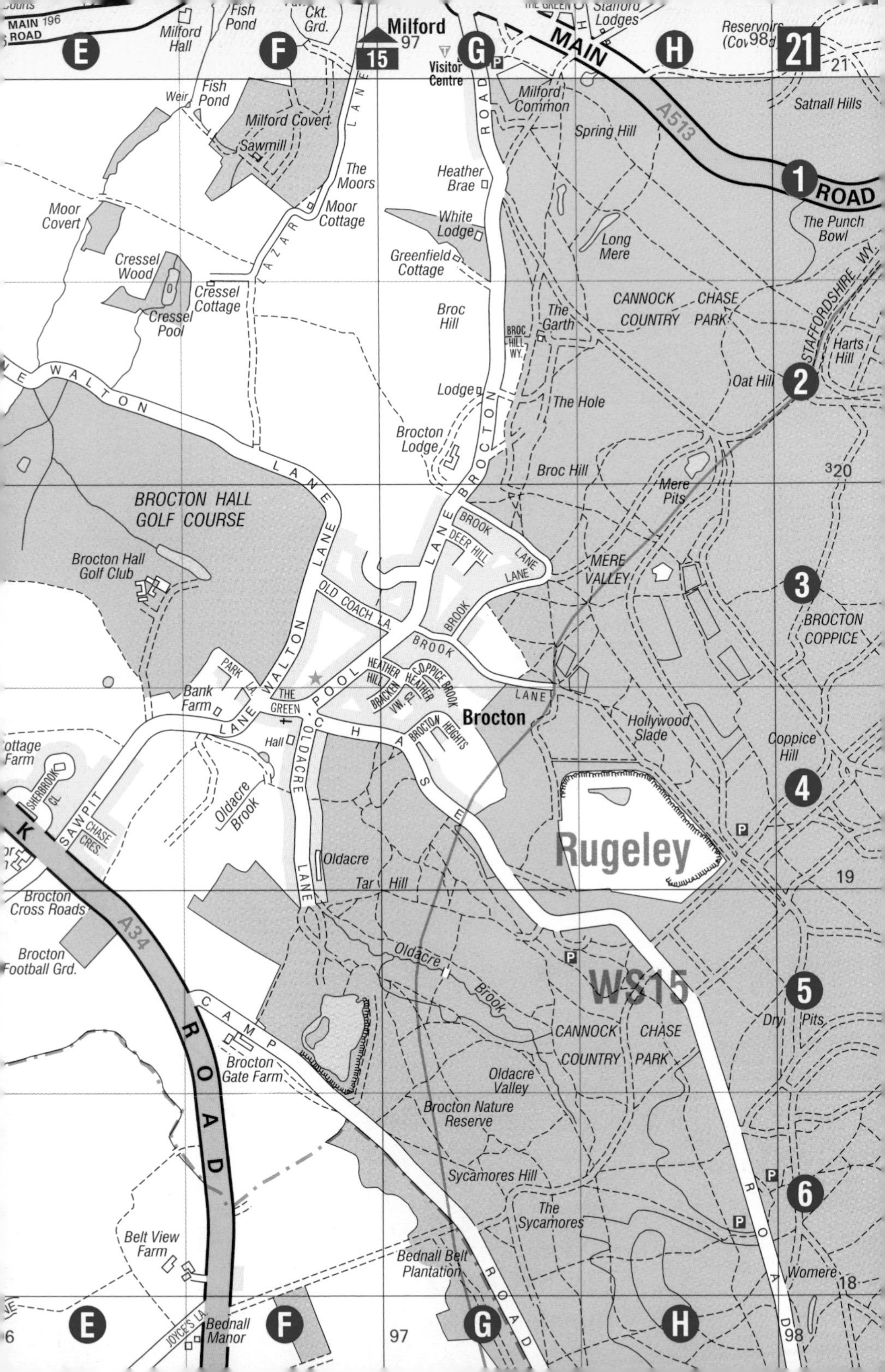
21
15
E
F
G
H
Milford
Milford Hall
Fish Pond
Ckt. Grd.
Visitor Centre
Stafford Lodges
Reservoirs
MAIN ROAD
Weir
Fish Pond
Milford Covert
Sawmill
Milford Common
Spring Hill
A513
Satnall Hills
The Moors
Heather Brae
Moor Covert
Moor Cottage
White Lodge
Long Mere
The Punch Bowl
Cressel Wood
Greenfield Cottage
LAZAR LANE
Cressel Cottage
Cressel Pool
Broc Hill
CANNOCK CHASE COUNTRY PARK
The Garth
STAFFORDSHIRE WY.
BROC HILL WY.
Harts Hill
Oat Hill
WALTON LANE
Lodge
The Hole
Brocton Lodge
BROCTON LANE
Broc Hill
Mere Pits
BROCTON HALL GOLF COURSE
BROOK LANE
DEER HILL
Brocton Hall Golf Club
MERE VALLEY
OLD COACH LA.
BROCTON COPPICE
PARK LA.
HEATHER HILL
COPPICE BROOK
HEATHER VW. CL.
BRACKEN
Bank Farm
THE GREEN
POOL
Brocton
Hollywood Slade
Hall
OLDACRE LANE
CHASE ROAD
BROCTON HEIGHTS
Coppice Hill
Cottage Farm
SHERBROOK CL.
SAWPIT
CHASE CRES.
Oldacre Brook
Rugeley
Oldacre
Tar Hill
Brocton Cross Roads
A34
Brocton Football Grd.
Oldacre Brook
WS15
CAMP ROAD
Dry Pits
CANNOCK CHASE COUNTRY PARK
Brocton Gate Farm
Oldacre Valley
Brocton Nature Reserve
Sycamores Hill
The Sycamores
Belt View Farm
Bednall Belt Plantation
Womere
JOYCE'S LA.
Bednall Manor
97
98
196
21
20
19
18
1
2
3
4
5
6

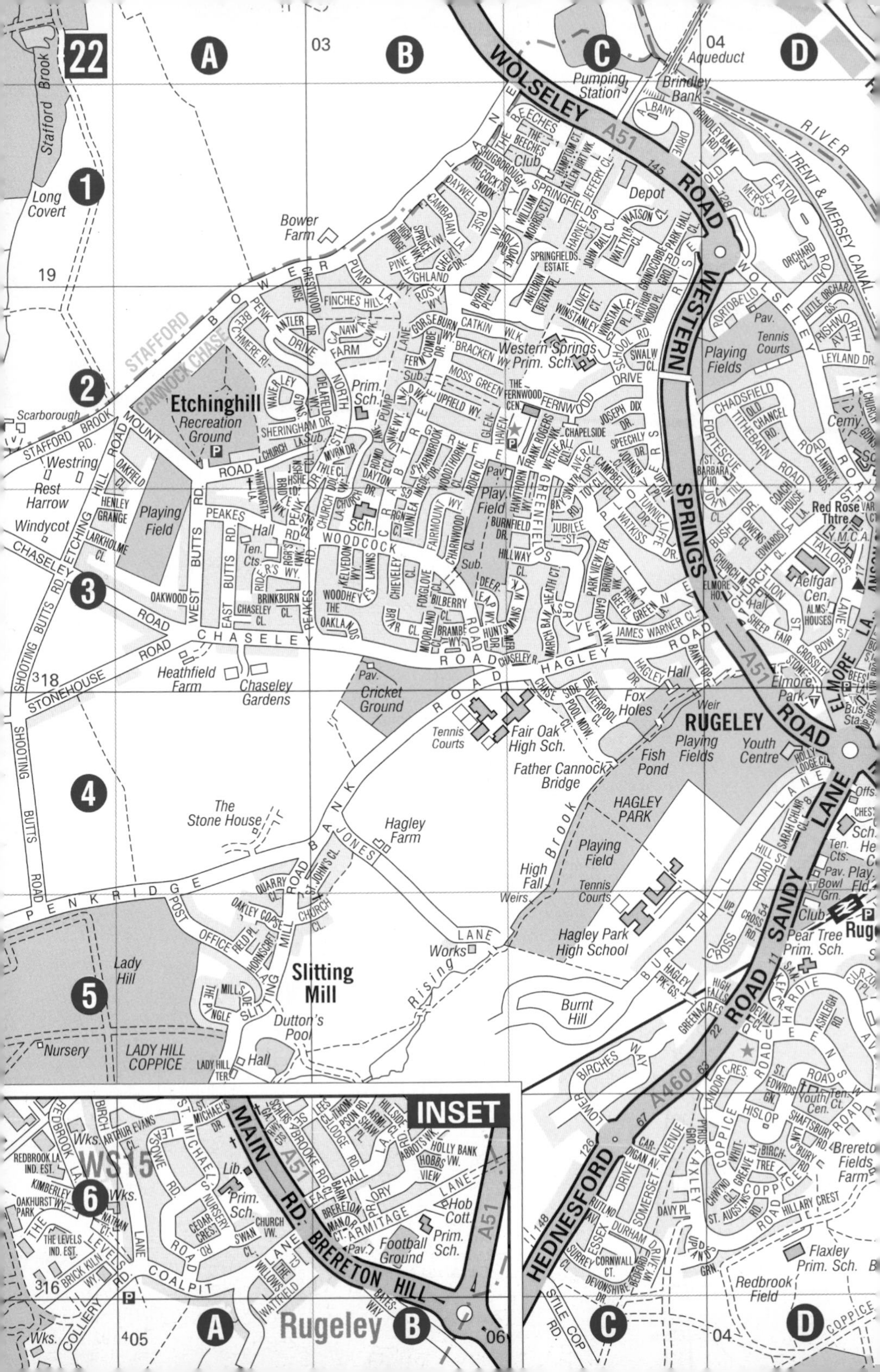

22
A
B
C
D
1
2
3
4
5
6
03
04
19
318
316
405
06
Aqueduct
Pumping Station
Brindley Bank
WOLSELEY ROAD
A51
RIVER TRENT & MERSEY CANAL
Stafford Brook
Long Covert
Bower Farm
Depot
Springfields Estate
Western Springs Prim. Sch.
The Fernwood Cen.
Playing Fields
Pav.
Tennis Courts
Cemy.
Red Rose Thtre
Y.M.C.A.
Aelgar Cen.
Alms. Houses
Elmore Park
Bus Sta.
STAFFORD BROOK RD.
CANNOCK CHASE
BOWER LANE
Etchinghill
Recreation Ground
Scarborough
Westring
Rest Harrow
Windycot
Playing Field
Prim. Sch.
Sch.
Play. Field
Hall
Ten. Cts.
CHASELEY ROAD
STONEHOUSE ROAD
SHOOTING BUTTS ROAD
Heathfield Farm
Chaseley Gardens
Cricket Ground
HAGLEY ROAD
Tennis Courts
Fair Oak High Sch.
Father Cannock Bridge
Fox Holes
Weir
RUGELEY
Playing Fields
Fish Pond
Youth Centre
HAGLEY PARK
High Fall
Weirs
Hagley Park High School
The Stone House
Hagley Farm
PENKRIDGE BANK
JONES LANE
Works
Rising Brook
Slitting Mill
Dutton's Pool
Hall
Lady Hill
Nursery
LADY HILL COPPICE
Burnt Hill
WESTERN SPRINGS ROAD
SANDY LANE
Pear Tree Prim. Sch.
Club
Pav. Bowl Grn.
Play. Fld.
HEDNESFORD ROAD
A460
Youth Cen.
Brereton Fields Farm
Flaxley Prim. Sch.
Redbrook Field
COPPICE
INSET
WS15
MAIN RD.
BRERETON HILL
Lib.
Prim. Sch.
Football Ground
Hob Cott.
Wks.
Rugeley

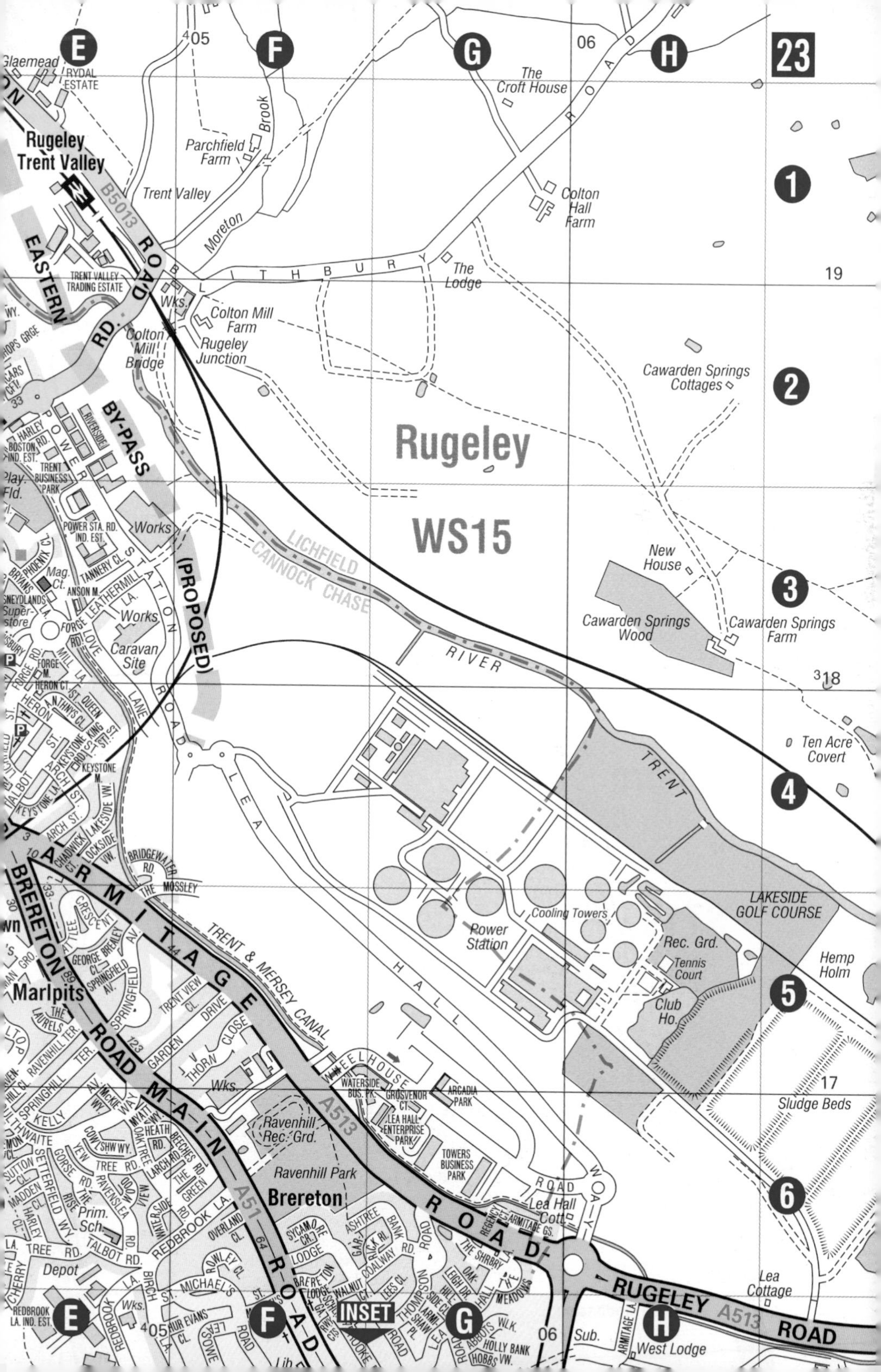
Rugeley
WS15
Rugeley Trent Valley
Trent Valley
Parchfield Farm
Moreton Brook
The Croft House
Colton Hall Farm
The Lodge
Colton Mill Farm
Rugeley Junction
Colton Mill Bridge
Cawarden Springs Cottages
New House
Cawarden Springs Wood
Cawarden Springs Farm
Ten Acre Covert
LICHFIELD CANNOCK CHASE
RIVER TRENT
Cooling Towers
Power Station
LAKESIDE GOLF COURSE
Rec. Grd.
Tennis Court
Club Ho.
Hemp Holm
Sludge Beds
Lea Cottage
West Lodge
Lea Hall Cott.
TRENT & MERSEY CANAL
ARMITAGE ROAD
BRERETON ROAD
MAIN ROAD
RUGELEY ROAD
A513
A51
B5013
EASTERN RD.
BY-PASS (PROPOSED)
Marlpits
Brereton
Ravenhill Rec. Grd.
Ravenhill Park
Prim. Sch
Depot
WATERSIDE BUS. PK.
GROSVENOR CT.
LEA HALL ENTERPRISE PARK
TOWERS BUSINESS PARK
ARCADIA PARK
TRENT VALLEY TRADING ESTATE
BOSTON IND. EST.
TRENT BUSINESS PARK
POWER STA. RD. IND. EST.
RYDAL ESTATE
Caravan Site
Works
Wks.
INSET
E
F
G
H
1
2
3
4
5
6
405
06
19
18
17

A
B
C
D
92
393
315
14
13
12
1
2
3
4
5
6
Grassmere Farm
Preston Fields
Preston Barn
Chase View
Longford Bridge
Longford House
LEVEDALE ROAD
STAFFORD ROAD
A449
PENK
WOODBANK LANE
Lock
Broom's Bridge
Penkridge Middle Sch.
Towing Path
STAFFORDSHIRE & WORCESTERSHIRE CANAL
RIVER
The Roller Mill
Flax Ovens
NURSERY DR.
COOKE CL.
CROCOTT CL.
STATION RD.
THE FLAX OVENS
UPLANDS CL.
GOODS STATION LA.
ROAD
LEVEDALE LANE
Riverside Farm
PRESTON VALE
PENK
Whiston Brook
Bull Bridge
STONE CROSS
STAFFORD CL.
TEDDESLEY ROAD
HATH. MILL HOUSE GS.
ERTON
FREDERICK RD.
KEMPSON RD.
LITTLETON
ORCHARD CL.
CRES.
LEACROFT RD.
ORCHARD CR.
LEACROFT RD.
M6
Sch.
The Marsh
Horse Fair
GROSVENOR CL.
MARSH LA.
PRESCOTT DR.
KENTMERE CL.
Penkridge Market
Cattle Market
LANE
CHURCH FM.
CHURCH RD.
ST. MICH'LS SQ.
CUTTLESTONE M.
CLAY ST.
CROWN BRI.
MILL ST.
MARKET ST.
BELLBROOK
HALING
Sch.
Lib.
THE SAPLINGS
CEDAR WY.
MKT. PL.
SAPLINGS CL.
HALING RD.
LITTLE MARSH PARK HOMES
LITTLE MARSH GRO.
CHERRYBROOK
HOLME RI.
WISCOMBE AV.
SHELSLY CL.
DRIVE
OAKLEY CL.
SPRGRS CL.
CANNOCK
NEW RD.
CROYDON
FRANCIS
Comm. Cen.
Penkridge Bridge
BRAMDEAN
ROAD
Football Ground
Penkridge
Cuttlestone Cottages
STATION RD.
LITTLETON MEWS
ST. MICHAEL'S CL.
Hlth. Cen.
ST. MICHAEL'S RD.
CHESTNUT GRO.
PENKRIDGE
PENKRIDGE WHF.
WESTWOOD DR.
KINGFISHER WLK.
GREENWAYS
CANNOCK RO
Tennis Courts
Wolgarston High Sch
Playing Field
Weir
PINFOLD
Cuttlestone Bridge
WHISTON RD.
TILDESLEY CL.
VALE RI.
DRIVE
GARDENS
GREEN LANE
DENEFIELD
Princefield First Sch.
SAXON
STREAMSIDE
ROAD
WULFRIC CL.
ATHSTN CL.
WAY
MOTORWAY
The Deanery No. 3 Holding
The Deanery
EATON LA.
BUNGHAM LANE
Nursery
MAYFIELD AV.
ELM WLK.
LIME WK.
GRANGE RD.
GRGE AV.
FALLOWFIELD CL.
MANORFIELD
HALING CL.
DENE CL.
LOCK RD.
PRINCEFIELD
PRINCEFIELD AV.
BARTLETT CL.
TEMPLARS
BRIDGEWR CL.
GREVILLE CL.
BITHAM CL.
EDWIN CL.
NORMAN
BROC CL.
ABBEY CL.
ELMDON CL.
ELWITH CL.
KEN.
Princefield
OTHERTON CL.
WHEATCROFT CL.
RENDMRE CL.
WOODTHRNE CL.
FILANCE
PILL.
WAY
FRANCIS CL.
B5012
WATER EATON LA.
The Deanery No. 8 Holding
BROOK CL.
BOSCO.
MOOR CL.
VALE
MANSTON
WATERBROOK
HILL
LANCE
ATON CL.
NEWLDS CL.
DRUIDS
KNIGHTS
BLOUNT CL.
WILGBY
MOOR HALL
M6
GRANGE CRES.
BOSCOMOOR LA.
WOLGARSTON
MICKLEWOOD
FULLMORE
ABLON CT.
WAVERDON
Stafford
WOLVERHAMPTON
Depot
BOSCOMOOR SHOP. CEN.
COMMERCE DR.
BOSCOMOOR IND. EST.
PENKRIDGE IND. EST.
CHETWYND
EGGIN DR.
PAGET CL.
COWLEY
MEADOW
TEVERAY
CANALSIDE CL.
CHELL
MODWENA
BRINDLEY CL.
The Deanery No. 7 Holding
Playing Field
Boscomoor
LYNE HILL IND. EST.
BOSCOMOOR LA.
Towing Path
WALHOUSE DR.
BEVERLEY CL.
ASTON CL.
BOYDEN CL.
WILLOW CL.
DRAKE AV.
HERON DR.
BEDINGSTONE DR.
MALLARD CL.
Warehouses
LANE
HILL
ST19
LYNE
Lyne Hill
The Poplars Farm
OTHERTON
WORCESTERSHIRE CANAL
LANE
Bridge House
Bramley Cottage
Nursery
Cape Cottage
FAIRFIELD DR.
Lynehill Bridge
Dairy Farm
Toyvale Cottage
MERE
The Willows
Otherton Farm
Otherton Bridge
Sub.
RODBASTON
Moat
Otherton
M6
MERE
DRIVE
LANE
RODBASTON DR.
Otherton Lane Bridge
A449
Rodbaston Stables
MICKLEY LA.
LANE
Rodbaston

INDEX

Including Streets, Places & Areas, Hospitals & Hospices, Industrial Estates, Selected Flats & Walkways and Selected Places of Interest.

HOW TO USE THIS INDEX

1. Each street name is followed by its Posttown or Postal Locality and then by its map reference; e.g. Acton Hill Rd. *Act T* ....5H **19** is in the Acton Trussell Postal Locality and is to be found in square 5H on page **19**. The page number being shown in bold type.
2. A strict alphabetical order is followed in which Av., Rd., St., etc. (though abbreviated) are read in full and as part of the street name; e.g. Avonlea Gdns. appears after Avon Hill but before Avon Ri.
3. Streets and a selection of flats and walkways too small to be shown on the maps, appear in the index in *Italics* with the thoroughfare to which it is connected shown in brackets; e.g. *Ballam M. Rug ....3D **22** (off Elmore La.)*
4. Places and areas are shown in the index in **blue type** and the map reference is to the actual map square in which the town centre or area is located and not to the place name shown on the map; e.g. **Brazenhill 5A 10**
5. An example of a selected place of interest is Ancient High House & Yeomanry Mus. 2E 13
6. An example of a hospital or hospice is KATHARINE HOUSE HOSPICE 1H 13

GENERAL ABBREVIATIONS

All : Alley
App : Approach
Arc : Arcade
Av : Avenue
Bk : Back
Boulevd : Boulevard
Bri : Bridge
B'way : Broadway
Bldgs : Buildings
Bus : Business
Cvn : Caravan
Cen : Centre
Chu : Church
Chyd : Churchyard
Circ : Circle
Cir : Circus
Clo : Close
Comn : Common
Cotts : Cottages
Ct : Court
Cres : Crescent
Cft : Croft
Dri : Drive
E : East
Embkmt : Embankment
Est : Estate
Fld : Field
Gdns : Gardens
Gth : Garth
Ga : Gate
Gt : Great
Grn : Green
Gro : Grove
Ho : House
Ind : Industrial
Info : Information
Junct : Junction
La : Lane
Lit : Little
Lwr : Lower
Mc : Mac
Mnr : Manor
Mans : Mansions
Mkt : Market
Mdw : Meadow
M : Mews
Mt : Mount
Mus : Museum
N : North
Pal : Palace
Pde : Parade
Pk : Park
Pas : Passage
Pl : Place
Quad : Quadrant
Res : Residential
Ri : Rise
Rd : Road
Shop : Shopping
S : South
Sq : Square
Sta : Station
St. : Street
Ter : Terrace
Trad : Trading
Up : Upper
Va : Vale
Vw : View
Vs : Villas
Vis : Visitors
Wlk : Walk
W : West
Yd : Yard

POSTTOWN AND POSTAL LOCALITY ABBREVIATIONS

Act G : Acton Gate
Act T : Acton Trussell
Arm : Armitage
Aston : Aston
Ast I : Astonfields Ind. Est.
Bed : Bednall
Bed H : Bednall Head
Bre : Brereton
Broc : Brocton
Colw : Colwich
Copp : Coppenhall
Cot H : Cotes Heath
Cot C : Coton Clanford
Derr : Derrington
Duns : Dunston
Ecc : Eccleshall
Gt Bri : Great Bridgeford
Gt Hay : Great Haywood
Hand : Handsacre
Hau : Haughton
Hixon : Hixon
Hopt : Hopton
Hyde L : Hyde Lea
Ing : Ingestre
L Hay : Little Haywood
Mars : Marston
Milf : Milford
Oul : Oulton
Penk : Penkridge
Ran : Ranton
Rug : Rugeley
Salt : Salt
Seigh : Seighford
Staf : Stafford
Staf T : Staffordshire Technology Pk.
Stone : Stone
Stone B : Stone Bus. Pk.
Tix : Tixall
Toll I : Tollgate Ind. Est.
Walt : Walton
West : Weston
Wol B : Wolseley Bridge
Yar : Yarlet

INDEX

A

Abbey Clo. *Penk* 3D **24**
Abbey Dri. *L Hay* 5F **17**
Abbeyfields. *Gt Hay* 3D **16**
Abbey St. *Stone* 3C **2**
Abbots Wlk. *Rug* 6B **22**
Abbots Wlk. *Staf* 6E **7**
Ablon Ct. *Penk* 4C **24**
Acton Ct. *Act G* 5F **19**
Acton Gate **4F 19**
Acton Hill **3B 20**
Acton Hill Rd. *Act T* 5H **19**
Acton Trussell **6H 19**
Adies All. *Stone* 3C **2**
Airdale Gro. *Stone* 1D **2**
Airdale Rd. *Stone* 1D **2**
Airdale Spinney. *Stone* 1D **2**
Albany Dri. *Rug* 1C **22**
Albert St. *Stone* 2C **2**
Albert Ter. *Staf* 6E **7**
Albion St. *Rug* 3D **22**
Aldbury Clo. *Staf* 2D **6**
Alder Gro. *Staf* 6B **12**
Aldershaw Clo. *Staf* 2C **6**
Aldersleigh Dri. *Staf* 2A **20**
Aldrin Clo. *Staf* 6H **7**
Alexandra Rd. *Staf* 4E **13**
Alexandra St. *Stone* 2B **2**
Allen Birt Wlk. *Rug* 1C **22**
Allendale. *Staf* 3B **6**
Alleynes Sports Cen. 1D 2
Alliance St. *Staf* 6C **6**
Alliss Clo. *Staf* 1H **13**
Alma St. *Stone* 2B **2**
Almshouses. *Rug* 3D **22**
Alsop Crest. *Act T* 6H **19**
Alstone Clo. *Staf* 4B **6**
Altona Clo. *Stone* 3D **2**
Amblefield Way. *Staf* 2C **6**
Ambleside Clo. *Stone* 3F **3**
Ampleforth Dri. *Staf* 5H **13**
Ancient High House & Yeomanry Mus. 2E 13
Anderton Vw. *Stone* 1A **2**
Aneurin Bevan Pl. *Rug* 2C **22**
Anson Dri. *Staf* 1D **20**
Anson M. *Rug* 3E **23**
Anson's Row. *L Hay* 5E **17**
Anson St. *Rug* . . . . 3D **22** (in two parts)
Antler Dri. *Rug* 2A **22**
Antom Ct. *Staf* 4F **7**
Apollo Cinema 3E 13
Appledore Clo. *Staf* 5C **14**
Appleyard Ct. *Staf* 2E **13**
Aqualate Ho. *Staf* 1E **19**
Arcadia Pk. *Rug* 5G **23**
Arch St. *Rug* 4E **23**
Arden Clo. *Rug* 2B **22**
Ardingley Av. *Staf* 4H **13**
Armishaw Pl. *Rug* 6B **22**
Armitage Gdns. *Rug* 6G **23**
Armitage La. *Rug* . . . . 6B **22** (in two parts)
Armitage Rd. *Rug* 4E **23**
Armstrong Av. *Staf* 6G **7**
Arthur Evans Clo. *Rug* 6A **22**
Arthur St. *Stone* 1C **2**
Arthur Wood Pl. *Rug* 2C **22**
Ascot Rd. *Staf* 4A **14**
Ashdale Clo. *Stone* 4C **2**
Ashdale Dri. *Staf* 3D **6**
Ash Dri. *Hau* 6D **10**
Ashflats **4E 19**
Ashflats La. *Staf* 4E **19**
Ashford Gro. *Stone* 4E **3**
Ashlands. *Hixon* 1H **17**
Ashleigh Rd. *Rug* 5D **22**
Ashley Clo. *Staf* 1A **12**
Ashridge Wlk. *Staf* 2D **6**
Ash Ri. *Staf* 3E **19**
Ash Rd. *Stone* 4D **2**
Ashtree Bank. *Rug* 6F **23**
Ashtree Clo. *L Hay* 5F **17**
Aspen Cft. *Staf* 5B **12**
Aston **1G 11**
Aston Bank. *Aston & Staf* 1G **11**
Aston Chase. *Stone* 3F **3**
Aston Clo. *L Hay* 5F **17**
Aston Clo. *Penk* 4C **24**
Aston Ct. *Stone* 1A **2**
Astonfields Ind. Est. *Ast I* . . . . 5E **7** (in two parts)
Astonfields Rd. *Ast I* 5E **7**
Astonfields Rd. Bus. Pk. *Staf* 5E **7**
Aston Hill. *Aston* 1G **11**
Aston Lodge Parkway. *Stone* 5F **3**
Aston Ter. *Staf* 5E **7**
Astoria Dri. *Staf* 1F **19**
Athelstan Clo. *Penk* 3D **24**
Attlee Cres. *Rug* 5E **23**
Attlee Cres. *Staf* 6C **12**
Auden Way. *Staf* 5C **12**
Augustine Clo. *Stone* 4E **3**
Austin Clo. *Stone* 4C **2**
Austin Friars. *Staf* 3E **13**
Avarne Pl. *Staf* 2E **13**
Avenue, The. *Stone* 2C **2**
Averill Dri. *Rug* 2C **22**
Averill Rd. *Staf* 5C **12**

Avon Clo. Staf 2H 13
Avon Gro. Stone 5D 2
Avon Hill. Staf 2A 14
Avonlea Gdns. Rug 3B 22
Avon Ri. Staf 2H 13

B

Babbacombe Av. Staf 5C 14
Bk. Browning St. Staf 1D 12
Back La. Hau 5D 10
Back La. Hixon 1H 17
Back La. L Hay 5E 17
Back La. Rug 3D 22
Back Radfords. Stone 3C 2
Badgers Cft. Ecc 1C 4
Badgers Cft. Staf 1A 20
Bagots Oak. Staf 6C 12
Bailey St. Staf 3E 13
Bakewell Dri. Stone 6F 3
Bala Ho. Staf 1E 19
Balk Pas. Staf 2D 12
Ballam M. Rug 3D 22 (off Elmore La.)
Balmoral Clo. Stone 5D 2
Balmoral Rd. Staf 4A 14
Bank Pas. Staf 2E 13 (off Market Sq.)
Bank Side. Stone 5B 2
Bank Top. Rug 3C 22
Barker Clo. Staf 2C 12
Barlaston Clo. Staf 3C 6
Barley Ct. Staf 6A 6
Barn Bank La. Staf 2C 18
Barn Clo. Rug 6B 22
Barn Clo. Staf 2E 19
Barnes Rd. Staf 6C 12
Barnfield Clo. Stone 4B 2
Barnfield Way. Staf 1A 20
Barnton Edge. Stone 1A 2
Baron's Way. Hixon 2H 17
Bartlett Clo. Penk 3C 24
Basil Clo. Staf 2F 19
Baswich 4B 14
Baswich Bus. Pk. Staf 3A 14
Baswich Crest. Staf 4B 14
Baswich Ho. Dri. Staf 6B 14
Baswich Ho. Way. Staf 6B 14
Baswich La. Staf 3B 14
Batesway. Rug 6B 22
Batholdi Way. Staf 5G 13
Baths La. Hixon 2H 17
Battle Ridge. Hopt 2B 8
Baxter Grn. Staf 1B 12
Bayswater Rd. Rug 3C 22
Baywood Clo. Staf 4A 14
Beacon Ri. Stone 5B 2
Beacon Rd. Stone 6C 2
Beaconside 1H 13
Beaconside. Staf 5G 7 (Sandon Rd.)
Beaconside. Staf 2C 6 (Stone Rd.)
Beaconside Clo. Staf 6G 7
Beaconside Sports Cen. 1B 14
Beaumont Gdns. Staf 5B 12
Bedford Av. Staf 2G 13
Bedford Way. Rug 6C 22
Bedingstone Dri. Penk 5C 24
Bednall 6D 20
Bednall Rd. Act T 6H 19
Beech Clo. Hau 6D 10
Beech Ct. Stone 3D 2
Beechcroft Av. Staf 3C 12
Beeches Rd. Rug 6F 23
Beeches, The. Rug 1C 22
Beechfield Dri. Staf 2B 20
Beech La. Copp 4C 18
Beechmere Ri. Rug 2A 22
Beechmount Ri. Staf 6A 14
Beech Rd. Ecc 2B 4
Beechway. Staf 5D 6
Beechwood Dri. Stone 5C 2
Bees La. Rug 3D 22
Beeston Ridge. Staf 6B 12
Belfort Way. Staf 5G 13
Bellasis St. Staf 5D 6
Bellbrook. Penk 2B 24
Bell Clo. Staf 6F 7
Belvedere Clo. Staf 5A 14
Benenden Clo. Staf 5H 13
Bentley Clo. Stone 1A 2
Berkeley St. Stone 1B 2
Berry Ring 6F 11
Berry Rd. Staf 4B 6
Bertelin Rd. Staf 4F 7
Betjeman Wlk. Staf 6C 12
Beton Way. Staf 3D 6
Betty Hatch La. Staf 6C 6
Beverley Clo. Penk 4C 24
Beverley Dri. Staf 3C 6
Bideford Av. Staf 5B 14
Bigwood La. Hyde L 3A 18
Bilberry Clo. Rug 3B 22
Billington Av. L Hay 4F 17
Billington Bank. Hau 6F 11
Billington La. Derr 3F 11
Birch Clo. Gt Hay 3E 17
Birch Clo. Staf 1D 20
Birches, The. Staf 6F 13
Birchfields Clo. Stone 5B 2
Birch La. Rug 6E 23
Birch Rd. Stone 3D 2
Birchtree La. Rug 6D 22
Birkdale Dri. Staf 1A 14
Bishops Ct. Ecc 1B 4
Bishops Grange. Rug 2E 23
Bishton La. Wol B 6H 17
Bitham Clo. Penk 3C 24
Blackberry La. Staf 1C 12 (in two parts)
Black Dri. Ing 5G 9
Blackheath La. Staf & Tix 6C 8
Blackhole La. Derr 3E 11
Blackies La. Stone 5F 3 (in two parts)
Blakiston St. Staf 1F 13
Blithbury Rd. Rug 1F 23
Blithfield Ho. Staf 1F 19
Blount Clo. Penk 4C 24
Blythe Rd. Staf 1E 19
Boardman Cres. Staf 3C 12
Boat La. West 1G 9
Bodmin Av. Staf 5B 14
Boningale Way. Staf 5B 12
Bonington Cres. Staf 3B 12
Boon Gro. Staf 1E 19
Boons Ind. Est. Derr 4G 11
Border Way. Staf 1E 19
Boscomoor 4B 24
Boscomoor Clo. Penk 4B 24
Boscomoor Ct. Penk 4B 24
Boscomoor Ind. Est. Penk 4B 24
Boscomoor La. Penk 4B 24
Boscomoor Shop. Cen. Penk 4B 24
Bostock Clo. Stone 6F 3
Boston Ind. Est. Rug 2E 23
Boundary Clo. Stone 6B 2
Bower La. Rug 2A 22
Bowers Ct. Stone 4F 3
Bow St. Rug 3D 22 (in two parts)
Boyden Clo. Penk 4D 24
Bracken Clo. Staf 3B 6
Brackenfield Way. Staf 3D 6
Bracken Vw. Broc 4G 21
Bracken Way. Rug 2B 22
Bradbury Ri. Staf 1A 12
Bradley La. Hyde L 2B 18
Bradshaw Way. Staf 3D 6
Bramall Clo. Staf 5C 6
Bramall La. Staf 5C 6
Brambleside. Staf 6A 14
Bramble Way. Rug 3B 22
Bramblings, The. Staf 1B 20
Bramdean Dri. Penk 2C 24
Bramhall Clo. Seigh 4D 4
Brandons, The. Staf 2F 19
Brandon Wlk. Stone 4B 2
Braunton Av. Staf 6C 14
Brazenhill 5A 10
Brazenhill La. Hau 5A 10
Brean Rd. Staf 6C 14
Brendon Clo. Staf 5B 14
Brereton 6A 22
Brereton Hill. Rug 6B 22
Brereton Lodge. Rug 6F 23
Brereton Mnr. Ct. Rug 6B 22
Brereton Rd. Rug 5E 23
Brewery La. Gt Hay 3D 16
Brewery St. Rug 4E 23
Briar Clo. Rug 3B 22
Briar Clo. Staf 1D 20
Briarsleigh. Staf 6A 14
Brickfield Clo. Hixon 1H 17
Brick Kiln La. Broc 4D 20
Brick Kiln La. Hopt 2B 8 (in two parts)
Brick Kiln Way. Rug 6A 22
Bridge Clo. West 1G 9
Bridge Cres. Stone 4C 2
Bridge St. Staf 2E 13
Bridgewater Clo. Penk 3C 24
Bridgewater Rd. Rug 4E 23
Bridle Rd. Staf 1B 20
Bridle Wlk. Rug 3A 22
Brindley Bank Rd. Rug 1D 22
Brindley Clo. Penk 4D 24
Brindley Clo. Stone 1A 2
Brindley Clo. Toll I 3F 7
Brinkburn Clo. Rug 3A 22
Brisbane Rd. Staf 4B 6
Broadeye 2D 12
Broad Eye. Staf 2D 12 (in two parts)
Broad Mdw. Cft. Staf 1A 12
Broad Oaks. Staf 2E 19
Broad St. Staf 2D 12
Broc Clo. Penk 3D 24
Broc Hill Way. Broc 2G 21
Brockton La. Walt 1D 20
Brocton 3F 21
Brocton Cres. Broc 4D 20
Brocton Heights. Broc 4G 21
Brocton Nature Reserve 6G 21
Brocton Rd. Milf 6G 15
Bromfield Ct. Stone 2C 2
Bromstead Cres. Staf 5B 6
Brook Clo. Penk 4B 24
Brook End. Hau 5D 10
Brookfield Ct. Hau 6C 10
Brookfield Ct. Stone 5E 3
Brookglen Rd. Staf 6E 13
Brooklands, The. Staf 3E 13 (off Friars' Wlk.)
Brook La. Broc 3G 21
Brookline Gdns. Staf 6A 6
Brookmead Ind. Est. Staf 3F 7
Brook Path. Stone 3B 2
Brookside La. Stone 4A 2
Brookside Pk. Staf 1H 11
Brook Sq. Rug 3D 22
Brookwillows. Staf 6A 14
Broomfield Clo. Stone 5D 2
Brooms Pk. Cvn. Pk. Stone 6D 2
Brooms Rd. Stone B 6C 2
Broughton Clo. Staf 4C 6
Browning St. Staf 1D 12
Browns Wlk. Rug 3C 22
Brundle Av. Staf 2B 12
Brunel Clo. Toll I 3F 7
Brunswick Ter. Staf 3D 12
Bryans La. Rug 3E 23
Buckingham Clo. Staf 4A 14
Buckland Rd. Staf 2D 6
Bull Hill. Staf 1E 13
Bull Ring, The. West 1H 9
Bungalows, The. Stone 4D 2
Bungham La. Penk 3A 24
Burcham Clo. Staf 4B 6
Burford Rd. Staf 4B 14
Burgage, The. Ecc 1B 4
Burlington Dri. Staf 5B 12
Burnett Ct. Staf 6A 6
Burnfield Dri. Rug 3B 22
Burnham Av. Staf 1B 20
Burns Av. Staf 5B 12
Burnthill La. Rug 5C 22
Bursley Clo. Staf 1D 18
Burton Bank La. Staf (ST17) 2E 19
Burton Bank La. Staf 2D 18 (ST18, in two parts)
Burton Ct. Staf 6E 13 (off Burton Sq.)
Burton Ho. Gdns. Staf 2E 19
Burton Manor 6E 13
Burton Mnr. Rd. Staf 1C 18
Burton Sq. Staf 6E 13
Bury Ring. Hau 6F 11
Bushberry Clo. Stone 5B 2
Bush Dri. Rug 3D 22
Butterbank La. Staf 2D 10
Butterhill Bank. Stone 6F 3
Butts, The. Gt Hay 4D 16 (Lichfield Dri.)
Butts, The. Gt Hay 5E 17 (Main Rd.)
Byron Clo. Staf 6G 7
Byron Pl. Rug 2B 22

C

Caernarvon Av. Stone 6E 3
Cairns Dri. Staf 6H 7
Caldervale Dri. Staf 1B 20
Camborne Clo. Staf 5C 14
Cambrian La. Rug 1B 22
Cambridge St. Staf 1G 13
Camelford Clo. Staf 5C 14
Cameo Way. Staf 4B 6
Campbell Clo. Rug 2C 22
Campion Clo. Ecc 3A 4
Camp Rd. Staf & Rug 5F 21
Canal Side. Act T 6G 19
Canalside Clo. Penk 4C 24
Canalside Rd. Stone 1A 2
Canaway Wlk. Rug 2B 22
Canberra Dri. Staf 1H 13
Cannock Chase Country Pk. 2H 21
Cannock Rd. Broc & Bed 3D 20
Cannock Rd. Penk 2C 24
Cannock Rd. Staf 6B 14
Canons Clo. Stone 5C 2
Cape Av. Staf 6B 12
Carder Av. Staf 4B 6
Cardigan Av. Rug 6C 22
Carisbrooke Dri. Staf 6B 12
Carling Clo. Staf 3B 12
Carlton Sq. Staf 5B 12
Caroline Ct. Ecc 2B 4
Carson Way. Staf 2C 12
Carver Bus. Pk. Staf 5E 7
Carver Rd. Ast I 5E 7
Castle Acre. Staf 6B 12
Castle Bank. Staf 5A 12
Castle Ct. Stone 5E 3
Castledene Dri. Staf 4C 12
Castlefields. Staf 3D 12
Castle Hill. Staf 2D 12
Castle St. Ecc 1B 4
Castle St. Staf 2D 12
Castletown 2D 12
Castle Vw. Derr 4G 11
Castle Vw. Staf 2D 12
Castle Vw. Est. Derr 3G 11
Castle Way. Staf 3C 12
Catalan Clo. Staf 5G 13
Catkin Wlk. Rug 2B 22
Cedar Cres. Rug 6A 22
Cedar Pk. Stone 3D 2
Cedars Dri. Stone 6D 2
Cedar Way. Staf 1D 20
Centre Rd. Stone 1A 2
Chadsfield Rd. Rug 2D 22
Chadwick Ct. Rug 4E 23
Chain La. Staf 2E 19
Chapelside. Rug 2C 22
Chapel St. Staf 2E 13
Chapel Ter. Staf 1E 13
Charles Cotton St. Staf 5C 6
Charlotte Clo. L Hay 5F 17
Charnley Rd. Staf 5F 7
Charnwood Clo. Rug 3B 22
Charterhouse Dri. Staf 4H 13
Chartley Clo. Staf 3C 6
Chartwell Rd. Staf 5A 14
Chase Cres. Broc 4E 21
Chaseley Clo. Rug 3A 22
Chaseley Rd. Rug 3A 22
Chase Rd. Broc & Rug 4F 21
Chase Side Dri. Rug 3C 22
Chase Vw. La. Copp 3C 18
Chatsworth M. Ecc 1B 4 (off High St.)
Chaucer Rd. Staf 5C 12
Chaulden Rd. Staf 2D 6
Cheadle Clo. Penk 4C 24
Chebsey Dri. Staf 5A 6
Chelford Clo. Penk 2D 24
Chell Clo. Penk 4C 24
Chell Rd. Staf 2D 12
Chelsea Way. Staf 3C 12
Cheltenham Dri. Staf 6H 13
Chepstow Dri. Staf 6A 14
Cherrybrook Dri. Penk 2D 24
Cherry Orchard. Stone 4E 3
Cherry Tree Clo. Ecc 1B 4
Cherry Tree Clo. Stone 6B 2
Cherrytree Cres. Gt Bri 1D 4
Cherry Tree Ho. Rug 6E 23 (off Setterfield Way)
Cherry Tree Rd. Rug 6E 23
Cherrywood Clo. Staf 1A 20
Chesham Rd. Staf 5F 7

Chester Rd. Ecc 1A 4
Chestnut Clo. Derr 3G 11
Chestnut Ct. Hand 4D 22
Chestnut Ct. Stone 1B 2
Chestnut Dri. Staf 2E 19
Chestnut Gro. Penk 2B 24
Chestnut Gro. Stone 1B 2
Chetney Clo. Staf 1B 12
Chetwynd Clo. Penk 4C 24
Chetwynd Clo. Rug 6D 22
Cheviot Dri. Rug 1B 22
Chieveley Clo. Rug 3B 22
Chiltern La. Ecc 2C 4
Chilwell Av. L Hay 6G 17
Christchurch Way. Stone 2C 2
Christie Av. Staf 3C 12
Christopher Ter. Staf 3G 13
Church Clo. Duns 6F 19
Church Clo. Hau 5C 10
Church Clo. Rug 5B 22
Church Clo. Staf 1F 19
Church Clo. Stone 3D 2
Church Cft. Gdns. Rug 2D 22
Chu. Farm Clo. Penk 2B 24
Churchfield Clo. Staf 4A 14
Churchfield Rd. Ecc 1A 4
Church Gro. Ecc 1A 4
Churchill Rd. Stone 4B 2
Churchill Way. Staf 2E 19
Church La. Derr 3G 11
Church La. Hixon 2H 17
Church La. Oul 1E 3
Church La. Rug 2A 22
(Mount Rd.)
Church La. Rug 3B 22
(Woodcock Rd.)
Church La. Staf 2E 13
Church M. Rug 3D 22
Church Rd. Hixon 2H 17
Church Rd. Penk 2B 24
Church St. Ecc 1A 4
Church St. Rug 3D 22
Church St. Stone 3C 2
Church Vw. Rug 6A 22
Clanford Clo. Staf 2F 19
Clanford La. Cot C 6C 4
Clanford Rd. Seigh 4C 4
Claremont Clo. Stone 3D 2
Claremont Gro. Staf 5B 12
Claremont Rd. Ecc 2B 4
Clarendon Dri. Staf 5B 12
Clare Rd. Staf 4C 6
Clark St. Staf 2F 13
Clay St. Penk 2B 24
Clematis Clo. Gt Bri 1D 4
Clement Clo. Staf 6F 7
Clevedon Av. Staf 6B 14
Cleveland Wlk. Staf 5B 12
Cliff Rd. Gt Hay 3E 17
Clifton Clo. Staf 2H 13
Clifton Dri. Staf 2H 13
Clinton Gdns. Stone 4C 2
Close, The. Staf (ST16) 4C 12
Close, The. Staf (ST17) 2E 19
Cloverdale. Staf 6A 14
Coach Ho. La. Rug 3D 22
Coachmans Clo. Staf 3C 6
Coalpit La. Rug 6A 22
Coalport Dri. Stone 5A 2
Coalway Rd. Rug 6G 23
Cocketts Nook. Rug 1B 22
Coghlan Dri. Staf 5C 12
Cole Dri. Staf 3C 12
Coleridge Dri. Staf 5C 12
Coley 3G 17
Coley Gro. L Hay 5F 17
Coley La. L Hay 5F 17
Colliery Rd. Rug 6A 22
Collingwood Ct. Stone 3D 2
(off Lichfield St.)
Colonnade, The. Staf 2E 13
(off Eastgate St.)
Colton Rd. Rug 1D 22
Colwich 6G 17
Colwich Cres. Staf 2A 14
Commerce Dri. Penk 4B 24
Common La. Stone 5A 2
Common Rd. Staf 2E 7
Common Rd. Ind. Est. Staf 3E 7
(Common Rd.)
Common Rd. Ind. Est. Staf 4E 7
(St Albans Rd., in two parts)
Commonside Clo. Staf 5D 6
Common Wlk. Staf 5D 6
Compton Clo. Staf 3F 13
Compton Rd. Staf 4B 14
Congreve Clo. Staf 6D 14
Conifer Gro. Staf 6B 12
Coniston Clo. Stone 4F 3
Coniston Ho. Staf 2F 13
Convent Clo. L Hay 6F 17
Conway Rd. Staf 1A 12
Cooke Clo. Penk 1B 24
Cook's Bank. Act T 6H 19
Cooksland 3D 4
Coombe Pk. Rd. Stone 6B 2
Co-operative St. Staf 5D 6
Cooper Clo. Stone 4F 3
Copeland Dri. Stone 6F 3
Cope St. Staf 2E 13
Coppenhall 3B 18
Copper Glade. Staf 2H 13
Coppice Brook. Broc 3G 21
Coppice Clo. Stone 2D 2
Coppice Gdns. Stone 2D 2
Coppice La. Rug 6D 22
Coppice Rd. Rug 6D 22
Coppice Rd. Stone 2D 2
Coppins, The. Staf 6A 14
Cornerways. Derr 3G 11
Cornwall Ct. Rug 6C 22
Cornwall Dri. Staf 4B 14
Coronation Rd. Staf 4F 7
Corporation St. Staf 6E 7
Corran Rd. Staf 1D 18
Coton Av. Staf 1H 13
Coton Clanford 2C 10
Coton La. Ran 1A 10
Cotters Hill Clo. L Hay 5F 17
Cotwalton 1H 3
Coulthwaite Way. Rug 6E 23
County Rd. Staf 1E 13
Courtland M. Staf 6F 7
Coventry Ct. Staf 6A 6
Covert Clo. Gt Hay 3D 16
Cowan Dri. Staf 1G 13
Cowley Clo. Penk 4C 24
Cowley Clo. Staf 5C 12
Cowlishaw Way. Rug 6E 23
Crabbery St. Staf 2E 13
Crab La. Staf 4B 6
Crabtree Way. Rug 3B 22
Craddock Rd. Staf 4C 6
Craftdown Clo. Staf 3F 19
Cramer St. Staf 3E 13
Cranberry Clo. Staf 5A 6
Cranbrook Wlk. Staf 5B 12
Cranmore Gro. Stone 4E 3
Cremorne Dri. Staf 6B 14
Crescent Rd. Staf 4D 12
Crescent, The. Ecc 2A 4
Crescent, The. Staf 1B 12
Crescent, The. Stone 2C 2
Crescent, The. Walt 6D 14
Crestwood Dri. Stone 5B 2
Crestwood Ri. Rug 1B 22
Creswell 3H 5
Creswell Dri. Staf 3H 5
Creswell Farm Dri. Staf 4B 6
Creswell Gro. Staf 2H 5
Crinan Gro. Staf 1C 18
Crispin Clo. Staf 3C 6
Croft Rd. Stone 5B 2
Croft, The. Hixon 2H 17
Crompton Clo. L Hay 5G 17
Crompton Rd. Stone 4D 2
Cromwell Clo. Hopt 3B 8
Crooked Bri. Rd. Staf 1E 13
Cross Butts. Ecc 2A 4
Cross Heads 6G 17
Crossing La. Derr 3E 11
Crossley Stone. Rug 3D 22
Cross Rd. Rug 5D 22
Cross St. Staf 6D 6
Cross St. Stone 2C 2
Crossway. Staf 2G 13
Crown Bri. Penk 2B 24
Crown St. Stone 3C 2
Croydon Dri. Penk 2B 24
Cull Av. Staf 2G 13
Cumbers, The. Seigh 4D 4
Curzon Pl. Rug 5D 22
Cuttlestone M. Penk 2B 24
Cypress Clo. Staf 4A 14

D

Daffodil Wlk. Rug 2B 22
Daimler Clo. Staf 5G 13
Danby Crest. Staf 5A 12
Danta Way. Staf 4A 14
Darnford Clo. Staf 3C 6
Dart Av. Staf 5B 12
Dartmouth St. Staf 2G 13
Darwin Clo. Staf 1A 14
Darwin Clo. Stone 1A 2
Daurada Dri. Staf 5G 13
Davies Clo. Staf 1G 13
Davy Pl. Rug 6C 22
Dawlish Av. Staf 6B 14
Dayton Dri. Rug 2B 22
Daywell Ri. Rug 1B 22
Deacon Way. Rug 2E 23
Deanery Clo. Rug 2D 22
Deanery, The 3A 24
Deanshill Clo. Staf 3C 12
Dearnsdale Clo. Staf 4B 6
Deepdales. Staf 1A 20
Deer Hill. Broc 3G 21
Deerleap Way. Rug 3B 22
Delafield Way. Rug 2B 22
Delamere La. Staf 5A 12
Dell Clo. Staf 3B 6
Dene Clo. Penk 3C 24
Denefield. Penk 3C 24
Denstone Av. Staf 4H 13
Denver Fold. Staf 5A 12
Denzil Grn. Staf 5A 12
Derby St. Staf 2D 12
Derrington 3G 11
Derrington La. Derr 4G 11
Derwent Av. Stone 4F 3
Derwent Ho. Staf 6E 13
Derwick Ind. Est. Broc 4D 20
Devall Clo. Rug 5D 22
Devonshire Dri. Rug 6C 22
Devon Way. Staf 1D 18
De-Wint Rd. Stone 4D 2
Dexton Ri. Staf 5A 12
Diamond Way. Stone 6D 2
Dickson Rd. Staf 6G 7
Dixon Clo. Stone 1A 2
Dobree Clo. Colw 6G 17
Dolphin Clo. Staf 4A 14
Dominic Ct. Stone 2C 2
(off Dominic St.)
Dominic St. Stone 2C 2
Dorrington Dri. Staf 5E 7
Dorrington Ind. Pk. Staf 5D 6
Douglas Rd. Staf 6G 7
Doulton Clo. Stone 5A 2
Doulton Rd. Staf 3H 7
Dove Clo. Staf 1F 19
Downderry Clo. Staf 5A 12
Downfield Gro. Staf 3D 6
Downing Gdns. Stone 4C 2
Downs, The. Staf 6A 14
Doxey 1A 12
Doxey Fields 1H 11
Doxey Fields. Staf 1H 11
Doxey Ho. Staf 1A 12
Doxey Marshes Nature Reserve 6B 6
Doxey Rd. Staf 1H 11
Drake Av. Penk 4C 24
Dreieich Clo. Staf 6F 7
Drive, The. Staf 1B 12
Druids Way. Penk 4C 24
Drummond Rd. Ast I 5E 7
Dryburgh Clo. Staf 6B 12
Dryden Cres. Staf 4C 12
Dunster Clo. Staf 6B 12
Dunston 6F 19
Durham Dri. Rug 6C 22
Dutton Way. Stone 6B 2

E

Eagle Cres. Ecc 2A 4
Earl St. Staf 2E 13
Earlsway. Gt Hay 3E 17
Easby Clo. Staf 6B 12
E. Butts Rd. Rug 3A 22
East Clo. Stone 4B 2
Eastgate St. Staf 2E 13
Eastlands. Staf 5E 13
Eastlands Clo. Staf 5E 13
Eastlands Gro. Staf 5E 13
Ebony Clo. Staf 1C 12
Eccleshall 1B 4
Eccleshall Rd. Gt Bri 1E 5
Eccleshall Rd. Staf 4A 6
Eccleshall Rd. Stone 6A 2
Edison Rd. Staf 6F 7
Edmund Av. Staf 4B 12
Edwards Clo. Rug 3D 22
Edwards Dri. Staf 2C 12
Edward St. Stone 2B 2
Edwin Clo. Penk 3C 24
Edwin Clo. Staf 5B 12
Eggington Dri. Penk 4C 24
Egg La. Hixon 2H 17
Elford Clo. Staf 3C 6
Eliot Way. Staf 4C 12
Ellington Av. Staf 1H 13
Elm Av. Staf 1D 20
Elm Clo. Gt Hay 3D 16
Elm Ct. Hyde L 2C 18
Elm Cres. Hixon 2G 17
Elmdon Clo. Penk 3D 24
Elmhurst Clo. Staf 3C 6
Elmore Ct. Rug 4D 22
(off Elmore La.)
Elmore Ho. Rug 3D 22
Elmore La. Rug 4D 22
Elm Rd. Stone 3D 2
Elmstone Clo. Staf 2C 20
Elm Wlk. Penk 3A 24
Elsdon Rd. Staf 1C 18
Elworthy Clo. Staf 6G 7
Embry Av. Staf 6G 7
Emerald Way. Stone B 6D 2
Epsom Clo. Staf 6A 14
Eremon Clo. Rug 6E 23
Ernald Gdns. Stone 4C 2
Espley's Yd. Staf 3E 13
Essex Dri. Gt Hay 2D 16
Essex Dri. Rug 6C 22
Essex Dri. Stone 6B 2
Essex Packhorse Bridge 3D 16
Etchinghill 2A 22
Etching Hill Rd. Rug 3A 22
Eton Clo. Staf 4H 13
Exeter St. Staf 5F 13

F

Fairfield Ct. Staf 5F 7
Fairfield Dri. Penk 5B 24
Fairmead Clo. Staf 1A 20
Fairmount Way. Rug 3B 22
Fairoak Av. Staf 3C 6
Fairview Way. Staf 5A 14
Fairway. Staf 2G 13
Fallowfield. Staf 1A 20
Fallowfield Clo. Penk 3B 24
Fallowfield Clo. Stone 5E 3
Falmouth Av. Staf 5C 14
Falmouth Clo. Staf 5C 14
Fancy Wlk. Staf 6D 6
Faraday Rd. Staf 6F 7
Farley La. Gt Hay 1E 17
Farm Clo. Rug 2B 22
Farmdown Rd. Staf 4A 14
Farrier Clo. Stone 4F 3
Featherbed La. Hixon 2H 17
Felden Clo. Staf 2D 6
Fellfield Way. Staf 3D 6
Fennel Dri. Staf 2F 19
Ferncombe Dri. Rug 2B 22
Fern Dri. Staf 1A 12
Fernhurst Clo. Stone 4E 3
Fernie Clo. Stone 5E 3
Fernleigh Gdns. Staf 6H 5
Fernwood. Staf 4D 6
Fernwood Cen., The. Rug 2C 22
Fernwood Dri. Rug 2C 22
Ferrers Rd. West 1H 9
Field Cres. Derr 3F 11
Field Ho. Ct. Stone 1B 2
Field Pl. Rug 5A 22
Field Pl. Staf 5E 7
Fieldside. Staf 2B 20
Fieldsway. Stone 3A 2
Field Ter. Stone 2C 2
Filance Clo. Penk 4C 24
Filance La. Penk 4C 24
Fillybrooks Clo. Stone 3B 2
Fillybrooks, The. Stone 2A 2
Finches Hill. Rug 2B 22
Firbeck Gdns. Staf 6A 14
Firs Clo., The. Staf 6B 14
First Av. Staf 3C 6
Firtree Clo. Copp 4C 18
Flax Cft. Stone 4D 2
Flaxley Rd. Rug 6C 22
Flax Ovens, The. Penk 1B 24

Fonthil Rd. *Staf* 5F 7
Ford Clo. *Stone* 4C 2
Forebridge 4F 13
Foregate Ct. *Staf* 1E 13
Foregate St. *Staf* 1D 12
Forest Clo. *L Hay* 5F 17
Forge M. *Rug* 3E 23
Forge Rd. *Rug* 3E 23
Forrester Rd. *Stone* 4D 2
Fortescue La. *Rug* 2D 22
Foxcote Clo. *Staf* 2C 20
Foxglove Clo. *Rug* 3B 22
Foxgloves Av. *L Hay* 6F 17
Fox Hollow. *Ecc* 2C 4
Foxwood Clo. *Stone* 5A 2
Francis Clo. *Penk* 3D 24
Francis Grn. La. *Penk* 2C 24
Frank Foley Way. *Staf* 1D 12
Frank Gee Clo. *Rug* 3C 22
Frank Rogers Wlk. *Rug* 2C 22
Fraser Clo. *Stone* 6B 2
Frederick Rd. *Penk* 2C 24
Freemen St. *Staf* 6E 7
Frew Clo. *Staf* 1G 13
Friars Av. *Stone* 4B 2
Friars' Rd. *Staf* 3E 13
Friars' Ter. *Staf* 3E 13
Friar St. *Staf* 6D 6
Friars' Wlk. *Staf* 3E 13
Frinton Clo. *Staf* 5F 7
Fullmore Clo. *Penk* 4C 24
Furlong Clo. *West* 1G 9
Furness Gro. *Staf* 6B 12

G

Gaol Butts. *Ecc* 2A 4
Gaolgate St. *Staf* 2E 13
Gaol M. *Staf* 1E 13
Gaol Rd. *Staf* 1E 13
Gaol Sq. *Staf* 1E 13
Garden Dri. *Rug* 5E 23
Garden Pl. *Staf* 3F 13
Garden St. *Staf* 3E 13
Garden Vw. *Rug* 3C 22
Garrick Ri. *Rug* 6F 23
Garrod Sq. *Staf* 6H 7
Garth Clo. *Staf* 2E 19
Garth Rd. *Staf* 2F 19
Gatehouse Theatre 2E 13
George Bailey Ct. *Staf* 4F 13
George Brealey Clo. *Rug* 5E 23
George La. *Stone* 4F 3
George St. *Staf* 6D 6
Gibson Clo. *Staf* 6F 7
Gillingham Cres. *Staf* 3B 12
Glade, The. *Staf* 5H 13
Gladstone Way. *Staf* 1H 13
Glamis Dri. *Stone* 6E 3
Glastonbury Clo. *Staf* 1B 20
Glebe Av. *Staf* 5D 6
Glebelands. *Staf* 1F 19
Glebelands Ct. *Staf* 2F 19
Gleneagles Dri. *Staf* 2A 14
Glenhaven. *Rug* 2B 22
Glen, The. *Stone* 4C 2
Glenthorne Clo. *Staf* 2B 20
Globe Av. *Staf* 1F 19
Globe Ct. Stone 3C 2
(off Newcastle St.)
Glover St. *Staf* 1D 12
Goodill Clo. *Stone* 6B 2
Goods Sta. La. *Penk* 1B 24
Gordon Av. *Staf* 4C 6
Gorsebrook Leys. *Staf* 6A 6
Gorseburn Way. *Rug* 2B 22
Gorse La. *Rug* 6E 23
Gorse Rd. *Rug* 6E 23
Gorsley Dale. *Staf* 1A 20
Gorsty La. *Cot C* 2C 10
Gough Clo. *Staf* 3C 6
Gower Rd. *Stone* 4D 2
Grange Av. *Penk* 3B 24
Grange Ct. *Hixon* 2H 17
Grange Cres. *Penk* 4A 24
Grange Rd. *Penk* 4B 24
Grange Rd. *Stone* 4E 3
Grange, The. *Hyde L* 2C 18
Granville Sq. *Stone* 2C 2
Granville Ter. *Stone* 2C 2
Grassmere Hollow. *Staf* 6H 5
Grassy La. *Hau* 5D 10
Gravel La. *Staf* 3F 19
Gray Wlk. *Staf* 6C 12
Great Bridgeford 1E 5
Great Haywood 3D 16
Greenacre. *Hixon* 1H 17
Greenacres. *Rug* 5C 22
Grn. Barn Ct. *West* 1H 9
Green Clo. *Stone* 4B 2
Greenfield Rd. *Staf* 1B 20
Greenfields Dri. *Rug* 3C 22
Greenfields Rd. *Hixon* 1H 17
Greengate St. *Staf* 2E 13
(in two parts)
Grn. Gore La. *Staf* 6D 14
Green La. *Cot C* 4B 10
Green La. *Ecc* 2B 4
Green La. *Hyde L* 3C 18
Green La. *Rug* 2B 22
Green Pk. *Ecc* 2B 4
Green Rd. *West* 1G 9
Greensome Clo. *Staf* 6A 6
Greensome Ct. *Staf* 1A 12
Greensome Cres. *Staf* 6A 6
Greensome La. *Staf* 6A 6
Green, The 3E 13
Green, The. *Broc* 4F 21
Green, The. *Milf* 6G 15
Green, The. *Rug* 6F 23
(in two parts)
Green, The. *West* 1H 9
Greenway. *Ecc* 2B 4
Greenway. *Staf* 2G 13
Greenway Av. *Stone* 5C 2
Greenways. *Hyde L* 2C 18
Greenways. *Penk* 3D 24
Greenwood Gro. *Staf* 6C 12
Greville Clo. *Penk* 3C 24
Grey Friars. *Staf* 6D 6
Greyfriars Bus. Pk. *Staf* 1D 12
Greyfriars Ct. Staf 6D 6
(off Marsh St.)
Grey Friars Pl. *Staf* 6D 6
Grey Friars Way. *Staf* 1D 12
Greylarch La. *Staf* 1A 20
Griffiths Way. *Stone* 5F 3
Grindcobbe Gro. *Rug* 1C 22
Grissom Clo. *Staf* 6G 7
Grocott Clo. *Penk* 1B 24
Grosvenor Clo. *Penk* 2C 24
Grosvenor Ct. *Rug* 6G 23
Grosvenor Way. *Staf* 1C 20
Grove Rd. *Stone* 3A 2
Guildhall Shop. Cen. *Staf* 2E 13
Gunnell Clo. *Staf* 3C 12

H

Haddon Pl. *Stone* 4F 3
Hagley Dri. *Rug* 3C 22
Hagley Pk. Gdns. *Rug* 5C 22
Hagley Rd. *Rug* 3C 22
Haling Clo. *Penk* 3C 24
Haling Rd. *Penk* 2C 24
Hallahan Clo. *Stone* 5E 3
Hall Clo. *Staf* 6G 13
Hall Farm Clo. *Hixon* 1H 17
Hambridge Clo. *Staf* 6D 12
Hammonds Cft. *Hixon* 2H 17
Hampton Ct. *Rug* 1C 22
Hanfords, The 3E 11
Hanyards La. *Tix* 2C 14
Harcourt Way. *Staf* 4B 6
Hardie Av. *Rug* 5D 22
Hardy Rd. *Staf* 5B 12
Hargreaves La. *Staf* 4D 12
Harland Clo. *L Hay* 5F 17
Harley Clo. *Rug* 6E 23
Harley Rd. *Rug* 2E 23
Harmony Grn. *Staf* 5B 12
Harney Ct. *Rug* 1C 22
Harris Rd. *Staf* 1H 13
Harrowby St. *Staf* 2G 13
Harrow Pl. *Stone* 4E 3
Hartland Av. *Staf* 6C 14
Hartlands Rd. *Ecc* 1B 4
Hartley Dri. *Stone* 2B 2
Hartsbourne Way. *Staf* 6A 14
Hartwell Gro. *Staf* 4A 6
Hatherton Rd. *Penk* 2C 24
Hatherton St. *Staf* 2G 13
Haughton 5C 10
Hawke Rd. *Staf* 4C 6
Hawkesmore Dri. *L Hay* 6F 17
Hawksmoor Rd. *Staf* 6E 13
Hawley Clo. *Stone* 6F 3
Hawthorn Av. *Stone* 6B 2
Hawthorn Clo. *Gt Bri* 1D 4
Hawthorn Clo. *Hau* 5C 10
Hawthorn Way. *Rug* 3C 22
Hawthorn Way. *Staf* 4G 13
Haybarn, The. *Staf* 4F 7
Haywood Ct. *Stone* 1A 2
Haywood Grange. *L Hay* 6F 17
Haywood Heights. *L Hay* 4F 17
Hazeldene. *Gt Hay* 3E 17
Hazel Gro. *Staf* 3C 6
Hazlestrine La. *Staf* 2A 20
Hazleton Grn. *Staf* 1D 18
Hearn Ct. *Staf* 6D 12
Heath Dri. *Staf* 4B 6
Heather Clo. *Broc* 3G 21
Heather Clo. *Gt Bri* 1E 5
Heather Clo. *Rug* 6E 23
Heather Hill. *Broc* 3F 21
Heathfield Av. *Stone* 4C 2
Heath Gdns. *Stone* 5B 2
Heath Rd. *Rug* 6E 23
Hednesford Rd. *Rug* 6C 22
Heenan Gro. *Staf* 2E 19
Helen Sharman Dri. *Staf* 6G 7
Helford Gro. *Staf* 5B 12
Helston Clo. *Staf* 4B 14
Hempbutts, The. *Stone* 3D 2
Hempits Gro. *Act T* 6H 19
Henley Grange. *Rug* 3A 22
Henney Clo. *Penk* 4C 24
Henry St. *Staf* 5F 7
Herbert Rd. *Staf* 4E 13
Heron Ct. *Rug* 4E 23
Heron Dri. *Penk* 5D 24
Herons Clo. *Staf* 6A 14
Heron St. *Rug* 4E 23
Heronswood. *Staf* 6A 14
Hesketh Rd. *Staf* 1D 18
High Chase. *L Hay* 5F 17
High Chase Ri. *L Hay* 5F 17
High Falls. *Rug* 5D 22
Highfield Clo. *Act T* 6H 19
Highfield Dri. *L Hay* 5F 17
Highfield Gro. *Staf* 6D 12
Highfield Rd. *Hixon* 2H 17
Highfields 6B 12
Highgrove. *Stone* 6E 3
Highlands. *Staf* 5D 12
Highlands. *Stone* 6B 2
Highland Way. *Rug* 1B 22
High Pk. *Staf* 4C 12
High Ridge. *Rug* 1B 22
High St. *Ecc* 1A 4
High St. *Hixon* 2H 17
High St. *Stone* 3C 2
Hilcote Hollow. *Staf* 5B 6
Hillary Crest. *Rug* 6D 22
Hill Cres. *Stone* 5C 2
Hill Crest. *Staf* 5C 12
Hill Cft. *Hixon* 2H 17
Hillcroft Av. *Staf* 6C 14
Hillcroft Park 6B 14
Hill Dri. *Stone* 5C 2
Hillfarm Clo. *Staf* 2F 19
Hillside. *Ecc* 2B 4
Hillside Clo. *Bre* 6B 22
Hillside Dri. *L Hay* 5F 17
Hill St. *Rug* 4D 22
Hilltop. *Rug* 5E 23
Hillway Clo. *Rug* 3C 22
Hinton Clo. *Staf* 1F 19
Hislop Rd. *Rug* 6D 22
Hixon 2H 17
Hixon Airfield Est. *Hixon* 1G 17
Hixon Airfield Ind. Est. *Hixon* 1H 17
Hixon Ind. Est. *Hixon* 2G 17
Hobbs Vw. *Rug* 6B 22
Hogan Way. *Staf* 1A 14
Holbeach Way. *Staf* 1B 12
Holdiford Rd. *Milf & Tix* 6H 15
Hollies, The. *Staf* 3D 12
Hollins Bus. Cen. Staf 6D 6
(off Rowley St.)
Holly Bank Vw. *Rug* 6B 22
Holly Dri. *Staf* 1D 20
Holly Gro. *Stone* 3D 2
Hollyhurst. *Staf* 2B 20
Holly La. *Cot C* 4A 10
Holly Lodge Clo. *Rug* 4D 22
Hollyrood Clo. *Staf* 2A 14
Holmcroft 5C 6
Holmcroft Rd. *Staf* 5C 6
Holme Ri. *Penk* 2D 24
Holmes Clo. *Staf* 3B 12
Holyoake Pl. *Rug* 1C 22
Holyrood Clo. *Stone* 5E 3
Homestead Ct. *Staf* 4E 7
Honiton Clo. *Staf* 5C 14
Hoomill La. *Gt Hay* 1C 16
Hopton 2A 8
Hopton Bank. *Hopt* 2A 8
Hopton Ct. *Staf* 6D 6
Hoptonhall La. *Hopt* 2A 8
Hopton Heath 2C 8
Hopton La. *Hopt* 2H 7
Hopton St. *Staf* 5F 7
Hornscroft. *Rug* 5A 22
Horse Fair. *Ecc* 1B 4
Horse Fair. *Rug* 4D 22
Horseshoe Dri. *Rug* 2A 22
Hoskins Ct. *Stone* 4E 3
Howard Rd. *Staf* 6E 13
Hunters Ride. *Staf* 3E 19
Huntsmans Wlk. *Rug* 3B 22
Hurlingham Rd. *Staf* 4B 6
Hurstbourne Clo. Rug 2B 22
(off Lansdowne Way)
Hurstmead Dri. *Staf* 2A 20
Hussey Clo. *Penk* 4C 24
Hutchinson Clo. *Rug* 2A 22
Hyde Ct. *Staf* 6D 12
Hyde Lea 2C 18
Hyde Lea Bank. *Hyde L* 2C 18

I

Ingestre 5H 9
Ingestre Rd. *Staf* 4E 13
Inglemere Dri. *Staf* 1A 20
Ingleside. *Rug* 3B 22
Inglewood. *Staf* 4D 12
Isabel Clo. *Staf* 5B 12
Island Grn. *Staf* 1B 20
Ivy Clo. *Act T* 6H 19
Ivy Cottage Mobile Home Pk. *Hopt* 1B 8
Ivy Ct. *Act T* 6G 19
Ivy Ct. *Hixon* 2G 17
Izaak Walton Clo. *Staf* 5D 6
Izaak Walton St. *Staf* 6D 6
Izaak Walton Wlk. *Staf* 3D 12

J

Jacobs Cft. *Staf* 4C 6
James Warner Clo. *Rug* 3C 22
Jasmine Rd. *Gt Bri* 1D 4
Jeffery Clo. *Rug* 1C 22
Jerningham St. *Staf* 2D 12
Jervis Rd. *Stone* 4D 2
John Amery Dri. *Staf* 1D 18
John Ball Clo. *Rug* 1C 22
John Donne St. *Staf* 5D 6
John Pershall Ct. Ecc 1A 4
(off High St.)
Johnson Clo. *Rug* 2C 22
Johnson Gro. *Stone* 4F 3
John St. *Staf* 1G 13
John Till Clo. *Rug* 3D 22
Jolt La. *Hau* 6C 10
Jones Clo. *Staf* 6D 12
Jones La. *Rug* 4B 22
(in two parts)
Jordan Way. *Stone* 4D 2
Joseph Dix Dri. *Rug* 2C 22
Joyce's La. *Bed H* 6E 21
Jubilee Ct. *Staf* 6F 7
Jubilee St. *Rug* 3C 22
Jupiter Way. *Staf* 5G 13

K

KATHARINE HOUSE HOSPICE. 1H 13
Keats Av. *Staf* 6C 12
Keep, The. *Staf* 5C 12
Keld Av. *Staf* 5A 12
Kelly Av. *Rug* 6E 23
Kelvedon Way. *Rug* 3B 22
Kempson Rd. *Penk* 2C 24
Kendal Clo. *Staf* 6B 12
Kenilworth Clo. *Penk* 3D 24
Kennedy Pl. *Ecc* 2A 4
Kennedy Way. *Staf* 3B 6
Kensington Clo. *Stone* 6E 3
Kensington Dri. *Staf* 2A 14
Kent Gro. *Stone* 1B 2

Kentish Clo. Staf . . . 5A 12
Kentmere Clo. Penk . . . 2D 24
Kentmere Clo. Staf . . . 5B 12
Kent Way. Staf . . . 5H 13
Kenworthy Rd. Staf . . . 5E 7
Kerry La. Ecc . . . 2A 4
Kestrel Clo. Staf . . . 4A 14
Keswick Gro. Staf . . . 5A 12
Keystone La. Rug . . . 4E 23
Keystone M. Rug . . . 4E 23
Keystone Rd. Rug . . . 4E 23
Kimberley Way. Rug . . . 6A 22
Kimberley Way. Staf . . . 5A 12
Kingcup Rd. Staf . . . 2E 19
Kingfisher Dri. Colw . . . 5G 17
Kingfisher Wlk. Penk . . . 3C 24
King's Av. Stone . . . 2B 2
Kingscroft. L Hay . . . 4F 17
Kings Dri. Hopt . . . 3B 8
Kingsland Clo. Stone . . . 4E 3
Kingsland Ct. Stone . . . 4E 3 (off Kingsland Rd.)
Kingsland Rd. Stone . . . 4E 3
Kingsley Clo. Staf . . . 5E 13
Kingsley Rd. Staf . . . 5E 13
Kingsmead Nature Area . . . 2F 13
Kingston Av. Staf . . . 1H 13
Kingston Cen., The. Staf . . . 2G 13
Kingston Dri. Stone . . . 5D 2
Kingston Hill . . . 2A 14
Kingston Hill Ct. Staf . . . 2A 14
Kingston Row. Staf . . . 2G 13
King St. Rug . . . 4E 23
Kingsway. Staf . . . 3C 12
Kirkstall Av. Staf . . . 6B 12
Kitlings La. Staf . . . 6D 14
Knight Av. Staf . . . 1G 13
Knights Clo. Penk . . . 4C 24
Knowle Rd. Staf . . . 1B 20

L

Laburnum Clo. Gt Bri . . . 1D 4
Lady Hill Ter. Rug . . . 5A 22
Lamb La. Stone . . . 5B 2
Lammascote Rd. Staf . . . 2F 13
Lancaster Rd. Staf . . . 5G 13
Lancing Av. Staf . . . 5H 13
Lander Clo. Stone . . . 4F 3
Landor Cres. Rug . . . 6D 22
Landor Way. Staf . . . 5B 12
Landstone Rd. Staf . . . 5G 13
Lanehead Wlk. Rug . . . 2B 22
Lane, The. Copp . . . 4B 18
Lanrick Gdns. Rug . . . 2D 22
Lansbury Clo. Staf . . . 5E 13
Lansbury Rd. Rug . . . 6D 22
Lansdowne Clo. Stone . . . 6B 2
Lansdowne Way. Rug . . . 2B 22
Lansdowne Way. Staf . . . 1A 20
Lapley Av. Staf . . . 4A 6
Lara Clo. Staf . . . 2B 12
Larchfields. Stone . . . 5D 2
Larch Rd. Rug . . . 6E 23
Larchwood. Staf . . . 2A 20
Larkholme Clo. Rug . . . 3A 22
Larkin Clo. Staf . . . 6C 12
Larksmeadow Va. Staf . . . 1A 20
Lauder Gro. Hixon . . . 2H 17
Laurel Gro. Staf . . . 6F 13
Laurels, The. Rug . . . 5E 23
Lavender Clo. Gt Bri . . . 1E 5
Lavender Lodge. Colw . . . 6G 17 (off Main Rd.)
Lawn Rd. Staf . . . 4D 12
Lawnsfield Wlk. Staf . . . 2C 6
Lawn, The. Staf . . . 1E 19
Lawrence St. Staf . . . 4E 13
Lazar La. Milf . . . 1F 21
Lea Cres. Staf . . . 6D 12
Leacroft. Stone . . . 4F 3
Leacroft Rd. Penk . . . 1C 24
Lea Grn. Staf . . . 3C 6
Lea Hall Enterprise Pk. Rug . . . 6G 23
Lea Hall La. Rug . . . 6B 22
Lea Hall Way. Rug . . . 4F 23
Leahurst Clo. Staf . . . 1A 20
Lea Rd. Hixon . . . 1H 17
Lea Rd. Stone . . . 5B 2
Leasawe Clo. Gt Hay . . . 3E 17
Leasowe Rd. Rug . . . 6A 22
Leathermill La. Rug . . . 3E 23
Lees Clo. Rug . . . 6B 22
Leese La. Act T . . . 6H 19
Legge La. Hixon . . . 1H 17
Leigh Clo. Staf . . . 2F 19
Leighswood. Staf . . . 6A 14
Lema Way. Staf . . . 2H 13
Lethbridge Gdns. Staf . . . 5A 12
Levedale Clo. Staf . . . 4A 6
Levedale Rd. Penk . . . 1A 24
Levels Ind. Est., The. Rug . . . 6A 22
Levels, The. Rug . . . 6A 22
Lexington Grn. Staf . . . 5A 12
Leyland Dri. Rug . . . 2D 22
Liberty Pk. Staf . . . 5A 12
Lichfield Ct. Staf . . . 3F 13
Lichfield Dri. Gt Hay . . . 4D 16
Lichfield Rd. Staf . . . 3E 13 (in two parts)
Lichfield Rd. Stone . . . 3D 2
Lichfield St. Rug . . . 4E 23
Lichfield St. Stone . . . 3C 2
Lilac Clo. Gt Bri . . . 1E 5
Lilac Gro. Staf . . . 6F 13
Lilleshall Way. Staf . . . 6B 12
Limedale Ct. Stone . . . 2B 2
Lime Tree Av. Staf . . . 6D 6
Lime Wlk. Penk . . . 3B 24
Linacre Rd. Ecc . . . 2B 4
Lincoln Mdw. Staf . . . 5A 12
Lindenbrook Va. Staf . . . 6A 14
Linden Clo. Staf . . . 5B 12
Lindens, The. Stone . . . 6D 2
Lineker Clo. Staf . . . 2B 12
Linksfield Gro. Staf . . . 3D 6
Lion St. Rug . . . 3D 22
Lion Way. Staf . . . 5G 13
Lister Rd. Staf . . . 6F 7
Little Haywood . . . 6F 17
Lit. Marsh Gro. Penk . . . 2C 24
Lit. Marsh Pk. Homes. Penk . . . 2C 24
Lit. Orchard Gdns. Rug . . . 2D 22
Little Stoke . . . 5E 3
Little Tixall . . . 3E 17
Lit. Tixall La. Gt Hay . . . 3D 16
Littleton Clo. Staf . . . 1G 13
Littleton Cres. Penk . . . 2C 24
Littleton M. Penk . . . 2B 24
Littleworth . . . 3G 13
Lloyd St. Staf . . . 1E 13
Locke Way. Staf . . . 2H 13
Lock Rd. Penk . . . 3C 24
Lockside Vw. Rug . . . 4E 23
Lodgefield Pk. Staf . . . 3B 14
Lodge Rd. Rug . . . 6F 23
London Rd. West . . . 1H 9
Longfield Av. Stone . . . 4B 2
Longhope Dri. Stone . . . 4B 2
Longhurst Dri. Staf . . . 1H 13
Long La. Hau . . . 4A 10
Long Mdw. Staf . . . 3E 19
Longshore Clo. Staf . . . 1C 18
Longton Rd. Stone . . . 2C 2
Lonsdale Ct. Ecc . . . 1A 4 (off High St.)
Lotus Ct. Stone . . . 1C 2
Lotus Way. Staf . . . 6F 7
Lovatt St. Staf . . . 6D 6
Lovelace Clo. Staf . . . 5C 12
Love La. Rug . . . 3E 23
Love La. Seigh . . . 3E 5 (in two parts)
Lovell Dri. Staf . . . 6H 7
Lovett Ct. Rug . . . 2C 22
Lwr. Birches Way. Rug . . . 6C 22
Lwr. Brook St. Rug . . . 3D 22
Lwr. Penkridge Rd. Act T . . . 6H 19
Loynton Clo. Staf . . . 4B 6
Ludgrove Way. Staf . . . 5H 13
Lymington Rd. Staf . . . 1A 14
Lyndhurst Gro. Stone . . . 5F 3
Lyne Hill . . . 5B 24
Lyne Hill Ind. Est. Penk . . . 4B 24
Lyne Hill La. Penk . . . 5A 24
Lynton Av. Staf . . . 6B 14
Lyric Clo. Staf . . . 1F 19
Lytham Dri. Staf . . . 2A 14

M

McKie Way. Rug . . . 6E 23
Madden Clo. Rug . . . 6E 23
Madford Retail Pk. Staf . . . 1D 12
Magnolia Clo. Gt Bri . . . 1D 4
Mahogany Dri. Staf . . . 1C 12
Main Rd. Gt Hay & Colw . . . 3D 16
Main Rd. Milf . . . 6E 15
Main Rd. Rug . . . 6F 23
Malcolm Rd. Staf . . . 1D 18
Mallard Av. Staf . . . 6G 13
Mallard Clo. Penk . . . 5C 24
Mallory Clo. Stone . . . 5D 2
Mallow Clo. Ecc . . . 3B 4
Malt Mill La. Staf . . . 2E 13
Malvern Clo. Staf . . . 4H 13
Malvern Dri. Rug . . . 2B 22
Manor Clo. Gt Hay . . . 3D 16
Manor Clo. West . . . 1H 9
Manor Ct. Stone . . . 5B 2
Mnr. Farm Cres. Staf . . . 2E 19
Mnr. Farm Rd. L Hay . . . 5F 17
Manorfield Clo. Penk . . . 3B 24
Manor Grn. Staf . . . 6D 12
Manor Ri. Stone . . . 4B 2
Manor Sq. Staf . . . 6D 12
Mansell Clo. Staf . . . 3C 12
Manston Hill. Penk . . . 4B 24
Mapledene Clo. Staf . . . 2B 20
Maple Dri. Derr . . . 3F 11
Maple Gdns. Stone . . . 5C 2
Maple Gro. Staf . . . 6E 13
Maple Wood. Staf . . . 2A 20
March Banks. Rug . . . 3C 22
Marconi Ga. Staf T . . . 6A 8
Margaret St. Stone . . . 2B 2
Marketfields. Ecc . . . 1B 4
Market Pl. Penk . . . 2B 24
Market Pl. Stone . . . 3C 2
Market Sq. Rug . . . 3D 22
Market Sq. Staf . . . 2E 13
Market St. Penk . . . 2B 24
Market St. Rug . . . 3E 23
Market St. Staf . . . 2E 13
Marlborough Av. Staf . . . 1A 14
Marlborough Clo. Gt Hay . . . 3E 17
Marlborough Rd. Stone . . . 6B 2
Marlowe Rd. Staf . . . 5B 12
Marlpits . . . 5E 23
Marsh Ct. Staf . . . 6D 6
Marsh La. Penk . . . 2C 24
Marsh St. Staf . . . 6D 6
Marsh, The . . . 2C 24
Marsland Clo. Staf . . . 1A 12
Marsland Rd. Staf . . . 1A 12
Marston Ct. Staf . . . 5E 7
Marston Dri. Staf . . . 6E 7
Marston Ho. Staf . . . 6E 7
Marston La. Mars . . . 1E 7
Marston Rd. Staf . . . 6E 7
Marston Rd. Trad. Pk. Staf . . . 5E 7
Marsworth Way. Staf . . . 2D 6
Martindale. Staf . . . 1B 20
Martin Dri. Staf . . . 2C 12
Martin St. Staf . . . 2E 13
Martins Way. Hixon . . . 2H 17
Mary Rand Clo. Staf . . . 5D 12
Masefield Dri. Staf . . . 5C 12
Matthews Rd. Staf . . . 6C 12
Maybank. Rug . . . 4D 22 (off Horse Fair)
Mayfield Av. Penk . . . 3B 24
Mayfield Rd. Staf . . . 4A 14
Mayflower Dri. Rug . . . 3B 22
Mayock Cres. Staf . . . 3B 12
Mdw. Bank Av. West . . . 1G 9
Meadowbank Ct. Stone . . . 5E 3
Mdw. Bank Wlk. Staf . . . 3C 6
Meadow Clo. Ecc . . . 1B 4
Meadow Clo. Penk . . . 4C 24
Meadow Ct. Staf . . . 5G 13
Meadow Dri. Hau . . . 5C 10
Meadow Glade. Hixon . . . 2H 17
Meadow La. Act T & L Hay . . . 6E 17
Meadow La. Derr . . . 3G 11 (in two parts)
Meadow Ridge. Staf . . . 5A 14
Meadow Rd. Staf . . . 5F 13
Meadows, The. Rug . . . 6G 23
Meadow Way. Stone . . . 5B 2
Meadway Dri. Staf . . . 2A 20
Meaford Av. Stone . . . 1B 2
Meakin Clo. Stone . . . 5E 3
Meakin Gro. Staf . . . 5B 6
Meakin Ho. Stone . . . 2B 2
Melbourne Cres. Staf . . . 6H 7
Melrose Av. Staf . . . 6B 12
Melrose Av. Stone . . . 6E 3
Mendip Av. Staf . . . 1C 20
Mercer Av. Stone . . . 4E 3
Mere La. Penk . . . 6A 24
Merrey Rd. Staf . . . 6E 13
Merrivale Rd. Staf . . . 6E 13
Mersey Clo. Rug . . . 1D 22
Meyrick Rd. Staf . . . 4E 13
Micklewood Clo. Penk . . . 4C 24
Micklewood La. Penk . . . 6D 24
Middle Friars. Staf . . . 3E 13
Milford . . . 6G 15
Milford Common Vis. Cen. . . . 6G 15
Milford Rd. Staf . . . 6C 14
Mill Bank. Staf . . . 2E 13
Mill Ct. Gt Hay . . . 2D 16
Mill Ct. Staf . . . 2E 13 (off Mill St.)
Millennium Way. Stone . . . 1A 2
Millers Ga. Stone . . . 3C 2 (off Christchurch Way)
Millhouse Gdns. Penk . . . 2C 24
Millington St. Rug . . . 2D 22
Mill La. Act T . . . 4F 19
Mill La. Gt Hay . . . 2D 16
Mill La. Rug . . . 3E 23
Millside. Rug . . . 5A 22
Mill St. Penk . . . 2B 24
Mill St. Staf . . . 2E 13
Mill St. Stone . . . 3C 2
Millwalk Av. Stone . . . 4E 3
Milton Gro. Staf . . . 6B 12 (in two parts)
Miss Pickerings Fld. Act T . . . 6H 19
Moat Ho. Dri. Hau . . . 5C 10
Moccasin Way. Staf . . . 5F 7
Montville Dri. Staf . . . 5B 12
Moor Clo. Act T . . . 5H 19
Moore Clo. Stone . . . 5E 3
Moorfields. Staf . . . 4D 6
Moor Hall La. Penk . . . 4D 24
Moorings, The. Colw . . . 6G 17
Moorings, The. Stone . . . 3C 2
Moorland Clo. Rug . . . 3B 22
Moor La. Seigh . . . 4E 5
Moreton Rd. Staf . . . 1D 18
Morland Clo. Stone . . . 6D 2
Morris Dri. Staf . . . 1A 14
Moseley Row. Hopt . . . 2A 8
Moss Grn. Rug . . . 2B 22
Mossley, The. Rug . . . 5E 23
Moss Pit . . . 2E 19
Mosspit. Staf . . . 2E 19
Mossvale Gro. Staf . . . 6A 6
Mount Av. Stone . . . 1B 2
Mount Cres. Stone . . . 1B 2
Mount Edge. Hopt . . . 2H 7 (in two parts)
Mount Ind. Est. Stone . . . 1B 2
Mount Pleasant. Derr . . . 3G 11
Mt. Pleasant Clo. Stone . . . 5F 3
Mount Rd. Rug . . . 2A 22
Mount Rd. Stone . . . 1A 2
Mount Row. Staf . . . 2E 13
Mount St. Staf . . . 2E 13
Mount St. Stone . . . 1C 2
Mount Vs. Stone . . . 2B 2
Myatt Way. Rug . . . 6E 23
Mynors St. Staf . . . 2G 13

N

Nagington Dri. Penk . . . 4D 24
Nanny Goat La. Stone . . . 2C 2
Nash Av. Staf . . . 5B 6
Nash La. Act T . . . 6H 19
Nathan Ct. Rug . . . 6A 22
Navigation Loop. Stone . . . 1A 2
Nelson Way. Staf . . . 1E 19
Newall Av. Staf . . . 6H 7
Newbury Clo. Staf . . . 6A 14
Newcastle Rd. Cot H . . . 1B 4
Newcastle Rd. Stone . . . 1A 2
Newcastle St. Stone . . . 2B 2
New Garden St. Staf . . . 3E 13
New Inn Row. Broc . . . 4D 20
Newland Av. Staf . . . 4D 6
Newlands Clo. Penk . . . 4C 24
Newlands Clo. Stone . . . 5B 2
Newman Clo. Stone . . . 4E 3
Newman Gro. Rug . . . 5E 23
Newport Rd. Ecc . . . 3A 4
Newport Rd. Gt Bri . . . 1E 5
Newport Rd. Hau . . . 5C 10
Newport Rd. Staf . . . 4B 12
Newquay Av. Staf . . . 5B 14
New Rd. Penk . . . 2B 24
New Rd. Est. Hixon . . . 1G 17

New Row. *Hyde L* 2C **18**
New St. *Staf* 6D **6**
Newton Rd. *Staf* 6F **7**
Newtown **4D 20**
Nicholl's La. *Oul* 1D **2**
Norbury Ct. *Stone* 3C **2**
Norfolk Way. *Staf* 6C **12**
Norman Rd. *Penk* 3C **24**
North Av. *Staf* 4D **6**
N. Castle St. *Staf* 2D **12**
Northcote Clo. *L Hay* 5G **17**
Northesk St. *Stone* 2B **2**
North Pl. *Staf* 6D **6**
North Walls. *Staf* 2E **13**
Nursery Dri. *Penk* 1B **24**
Nursery La. *Staf* 6D **6**
Nursery Rd. *Rug* 6A **22**
Nursery Way. *Gt Hay* 2D **16**

O

Oak Av. *Staf* 1D **20**
Oak Clo. *Gt Hay* 4E **17**
Oakfield Clo. *Rug* 2A **22**
Oak Gdns. *Hau* 5D **10**
Oakhurst Pk. *Rug* 6A **22**
Oaklands Dri. *Staf* 4D **12**
Oaklands, The. *Rug* 3B **22**
Oakleigh Ct. *Stone* 5F **3**
Oakleigh Dri. *Rug* 6G **23**
Oakley Clo. *Penk* 2D **24**
Oakley Copse. *Rug* 5A **22**
Oakridge Clo. *Staf* 2C **20**
Oakridge Way. *Staf* 2C **20**
Oak Rd. *Ecc* 2A **4**
Oak Rd. *Stone* 3D **2**
Oaks, The. *Staf* 6D **14**
Oak Tree Clo. *Staf* 6B **12**
Oaktree Rd. *Rug* 6E **23**
Oakwood. *Rug* 3A **22**
Oddfellows. Stone 3C 2
(off Adies All.)
Oldacre La. *Broc* 4F **21**
Old Chancel Rd. *Rug* 2D **22**
Old Coach La. *Broc* 3F **21**
Old Cft. Rd. *Staf* 2C **20**
Old Eaton Rd. *Rug* 1D **22**
Oldfield Dri. *Stone* 5E **3**
Oldfields Cres. *Gt Hay* 3E **17**
Oldfields La. *Gt Hay* 2E **17**
Oldford La. *Cot C* 1D **10**
Oldhill La. *Tix* 4H **15**
Old Rectory Rd. *Stone* 3D **2**
Old Rickerscote La.
Staf 2F **19**
Old Rd. *Stone* 2C **2**
Old Rd. *West* 1H **9**
Old Rd. Clo. *Stone* 1C **2**
Old School Clo. *West* 1H **9**
Oliver Ho. *Stone* 4A **2**
One Oak Ri. *Staf* 2F **19**
Opal Way. *Stone B* 6B **2**
Opel Bus. Cen. *Stone* 6C **2**
Orchard Cvn. Pk. *Hopt* 1A **8**
Orchard Clo. *Oul* 4B **2**
Orchard Clo. *Penk* 2C **24**
Orchard Clo. *Rug* 1D **22**
Orchard Cres. *Penk* 2C **24**
Orchard La. *Hyde L* 2C **18**
Orchard St. *Staf* 3E **13**
Orchard, The. *Hopt* 1A **8**
Orchard, The. *L Hay* 5E **17**
Orwell Dri. *Staf* 5B **12**
Osborne Cres. *Staf* 5A **14**
Otherton **5C 24**
Otherton Clo. *Penk* 3B **24**
Otherton La. *Penk* 5C **24**
Otterburn Clo. *Staf* 1B **20**
Oultoncross **1C 2**
Oulton M. *Stone* 2C **2**
Oulton Rd. *Stone* 2C **2**
Oulton Way. *Staf* 5B **6**
Outwoods Clo. *West* 1H **9**
Outwoods Grn. *West* 1H **9**
Ovalside Ct. *Staf* 3F **13**
Oval, The. *Staf* 3F **13**
Overhill Rd. *Staf* 1B **20**
Overland Clo. *Bre* 6F **23**
Overpool Clo. *Rug* 4C **22**
Owens Clo. *Rug* 3D **22**
Owen Wlk. *Staf* 6C **12**
Oxbarn Rd. *Staf* 1D **18**
Oxford Gdns. *Staf* 6E **7**
Oxleathers Ct. *Staf* 6B **12**

P

Paddock Clo. *Staf* 4B **6**
Paddock, The. *Seigh* 5E **5**
Paddock, The. *Stone* 5F **3**
Padstow Dri. *Staf* 4C **14**
Paget Clo. *L Hay* 5G **17**
Paget Clo. *Penk* 4D **24**
Palmbourne Ind. Pk. *Staf* 2D **12**
Palmer Clo. *Staf* 1H **13**
Panton Clo. *Staf* 1H **13**
Pantulf Clo. *Staf* 4B **12**
Park Av. *Staf* 5D **12**
Park Av. *Stone* 3A **2**
Park Cres. *Staf* 4E **13**
Parker's Cft. Rd. *Staf* 3E **13**
Parkfield Bus. Cen. Staf 3E 13
(off Wolverhampton Rd.)
Parkfields. *Staf* 5D **12**
Pk. Hall Clo. *Rug* 1C **22**
Park Ho. Rug 3D 22
(off Crossley Stone)
Park Ho. Dri. *Stone* 4E **3**
Park La. *Broc* 3F **21**
Park La. *Hau* 6C **10**
Parkside **3D 6**
Parkside Av. *Staf* 2C **6**
Parkside Shop. Cen. *Staf* 3D **6**
Park St. *Staf* 3E **13**
Park Vw. *West* 1G **9**
Pk. View Ter. *Rug* 3C **22**
Parkway. *Stone* 4E **3**
Peach Av. *Staf* 1F **19**
Peakes Rd. *Rug* 3A **22**
Pearson Dri. *Stone* 3E **3**
Peel St. *Staf* 2D **12**
Peel Ter. *Staf* 6E **7**
Pellfield Ct. *West* 1H **9**
Pembroke Dri. *Stone* 4E **3**
Penk Dri. N. *Rug* 2A **22**
Penk Dri. S. *Rug* 3A **22**
Penkridge **2B 24**
Penkridge Bank Rd. *Rug* 5A **22**
Penkridge Ind. Est. *Penk* 4B **24**
Penkridge Wharf. *Penk* 3C **24**
Penkvale Rd. *Staf* 1F **19**
Penn Cft. *L Hay* 5F **17**
Penny Bank Ct. Rug 3D 22
(off Anson St.)
Pennycrofts. *Staf* 2F **13**
Pennycrofts Ct. *Staf* 2F **13**
Penzance Way. *Staf* 4C **14**
Perle Brook. *Ecc* 1A **4**
Perrin Clo. *Staf* 1F **19**
Peter James Ct. *Staf* 6E **7**
Phillips Clo. *Stone* 4F **3**
Phoenix Clo. *Rug* 3E **23**
Pike Clo. *Staf* 6G **7**
Pilgrim Pl. *Staf* 3E **13**
Pilgrim St. *Staf* 3E **13**
Pillaton Clo. *Penk* 4C **24**
Pine Cres. *Staf* 1D **20**
Pine Vw. *Rug* 1B **22**
Pinewood Dri. *L Hay* 5F **17**
Pinfold La. *Penk* 3A **24**
Pinfold Ter. *L Hay* 5E **17**
Pingle La. *Bed* 6D **20**
Pingle La. *Stone* 4D **2**
Pingle, The. *Rug* 5A **22**
Pintail Clo. *Staf* 6G **13**
Pippins, The. *Staf* 2E **19**
Pirehill La. *Stone* 6B **2**
Pitstone Clo. *Staf* 2D **6**
Pitt St. *Staf* 5C **6**
Plant Cres. *Staf* 6F **13**
Plovers Ri. *Rug* 3C **22**
Pool La. *Broc* 4F **21**
Pool Mdw. Clo. *Rug* 4C **22**
Pope Gdns. *Staf* 6C **12**
Poplar Clo. *Ecc* 2B **4**
Poplar Clo. *Hau* 5C **10**
Poplar Clo. *Stone* 4B **2**
Poplar Way. *Staf* 1E **19**
Porlock Av. *Staf* 5B **14**
Portal Rd. *Staf* 6H **7**
Portleven Clo. *Staf* 6C **14**
Portobello. *Rug* 2D **22**
Post Office La. *Rug* 5A **22**
Power Sta. Rd. *Rug* 2E **23**
Power Sta. Rd. Ind. Est. *Rug* . . 3E **23**
Prescott Av. *Staf* 1G **13**
Prescott Dri. *Penk* 2D **24**
Preston Va. La. *Penk* 2A **24**
Prestwood Ct. *Staf* 4E **13**
Prince Av. *Hau* 6D **10**
Princefield **3C 24**
Princefield Av. *Penk* 3C **24**
Princess Pl. *Staf* 6E **7**
Princes St. *Staf* 2E **13**
Prince's St. *Stone* 1C **2**
Priory Dri. *L Hay* 5F **17**
Priory Rd. *Rug* 6B **22**
Priory Rd. *Stone* 3D **2**
Priory Wlk. *Stone* 4D **2**
Prospect Rd. *Staf* 1F **13**
Puddle Hill. *Hixon* 1H **17**
Pulteney Dri. *Staf* 5B **6**
Pump La. *Rug* 1B **22**
Pyrus Gro. *Rug* 6C **22**

Q

Quarry Clo. *Rug* 4A **22**
Queen's Sq. *Stone* 1C **2**
Queen St. *Rug* 4E **23**
Queensville **5H 13**
Queensville. *Staf* 4G **13**
(in two parts)
Queensville Av. *Staf* 4G **13**
Queensville Bri. *Staf* 4G **13**
Queensville Retail Pk. *Staf* 4G **13**
Queensway. *Rug* 5D **22**
Queensway. *Staf* 1E **13**

R

Radford Bank. *Staf* 5H **13**
Radford Clo. *Stone* 2C **2**
Radford Ri. *Staf* 5A **14**
Radford St. *Stone* 2C **2**
Radstock Clo. *Staf* 1B **20**
Railway Cotts. *Colw* 6F **17**
Railway Cotts. *Gt Bri* 1E **5**
Railway Cotts. *Rug* 6A **22**
Railway St. *Staf* 2D **12**
Railway Ter. *Milf* 6G **15**
Ralph Ct. *Staf* 5B **12**
Rambleford Way. *Staf* 3D **6**
Rangeley Vw. *Stone* 1A **2**
Ranger's Wlk. *Rug* 3A **22**
Ravenhill Clo. *Rug* 5E **23**
Ravenhill Ter. *Rug* 5E **23**
Ravensbank Pk. Mobile Home Pk.
Hopt 1B **8**
Ravenslea Rd. *Rug* 6E **23**
Ravenswood Crest. *Staf* 6A **14**
Read Av. *Staf* 6F **7**
Reason Rd. *Staf* 2E **19**
Rectory Ct. *Staf* 3D **12**
Rectory La. *Hau* 5D **10**
Redbrook La. *Rug* 6A **22**
(in two parts)
Redbrook La. Ind. Est. *Rug* . . . 6E **23**
Redfern Rd. *Stone* 6B **2**
Redgrave Dri. *Staf* 2B **12**
Redhill **2C 4**
Redhill. *Staf* 3C **6**
Redhill Gdns. *Stone* 3D **2**
Redhill Gorse. *Staf* 3C **6**
Redhill Rd. *Stone* 3D **2**
Redhills. *Ecc* 2C **4**
Redlands, The. *Stone* 4E **3**
Red Lion St. *Staf* 1E **13**
Redmond Clo. *Rug* 2B **22**
Red Rose Theatre **3D 22**
Redruth Dri. *Staf* 4B **14**
Redwood Av. *Stone* 5D **2**
Regency Ct. *Rug* 6G **23**
Regent St. *Oul* 2B **2**
Rendel Gro. *Stone* 1A **2**
Rendermore Clo. *Penk* 3B **24**
Repton Clo. *Staf* 4H **13**
Reva Rd. *Staf* 5E **13**
Rhein Way. *Staf* 5G **13**
Richards Av. *Staf* 1G **13**
Richfield La. *Bed* 6D **20**
Richmond Clo. *Staf* 6E **13**
Richmond Gro. *Stone* 4C **2**
Richmond Pk. *Rug* 6A **22**
Rickerscote **1F 19**
Rickerscote Av. *Staf* 1G **19**
Rickerscote Hall La. *Staf* 2G **19**
Rickerscote Rd. *Staf* 1E **19**
Rider's Way. *Rug* 3A **22**
Ridge Cft. *Stone* 4E **3**
Ridgemont Ct. *Stone* 4E **3**
Ridgeway. *Hixon* 2H **17**
Ridgeway Clo. *Hopt* 3A **8**
Ridgeway Clo. *Hyde L* 2C **18**
Ridgeway, The. *Staf* 6A **6**
Rimbach Dri. *L Hay* 5F **17**
Ring, The. *L Hay* 4E **17**
Ripon Dri. *Staf* 6A **14**
Rise, The. *Rug* 6E **23**
Rise, The. *Staf* 6C **14**
Rishworth Av. *Rug* 2D **22**
Rising Brook **1E 19**
Rising Brook. *Staf* 6E **13**
Riverside. *Rug* 2E **23**
Riverside. *Staf* 2E **13**
Riverside Gro. *Stone* 2B **2**
Riverside Recreation Cen. . . . **2F 13**
Riversmeade Way. *Staf* 6A **6**
Riverway. *Staf* 3F **13**
River Way. *Stone* 4C **2**
Robinswood. *Staf* 1A **20**
Rockeries, The. *Staf* 1G **19**
Rockhouse Dri. *Gt Hay* 4D **16**
Rodbaston **6A 24**
Rodbaston Dri. *Penk* 6A **24**
(in two parts)
Roedean Av. *Staf* 5H **13**
Romford Mdw. *Ecc* 2A **4**
Romford Rd. *Staf* 5E **7**
Romney Dri. *Staf* 1B **12**
Rookswood Copse. *Staf* 1A **20**
Roseford La. *Act T* 4G **19**
Rose Hill. *Staf* 2C **12**
Rosemary Av. *Staf* 2F **19**
Rose Way. *Rug* 2B **22**
Rosewood Gdns. *Staf* 2C **12**
Rotherwood Dri. *Staf* 4C **12**
Rouse Clo. *Staf* 3B **12**
Rowan Clo. *Stone* 5D **2**
Rowan Glade. *Staf* 1A **20**
ROWLEY HALL HOSPITAL . . . **5D 12**
Rowley Av. *Staf* 4D **12**
Rowley Bank. *Staf* 5E **13**
Rowley Bank Gdns. *Staf* 5E **13**
Rowley Bank Ho. Staf 5E 13
(off Rowley Bank)
Rowley Clo. *Rug* 6F **23**
Rowley Gro. *Staf* 4E **13**
Rowley Hall Clo. *Staf* 5D **12**
Rowley Hall Dri. *Staf* 5C **12**
Rowley Park **5D 12**
Rowley Park Sports Cen. . . . **5D 12**
Rowley St. *Staf* 6D **6**
Royds Clo. *Hau* 5C **10**
Rudyard Clo. *Stone* 1A **2**
Rudyard Ho. *Staf* 1E **19**
Ruffin Ct. *Stone* 4E **3**
Rugeley **3D 22**
Rugeley Eastern By-Pass.
Rug 1D **22**
Rugeley Rd. *Arm* 6H **23**
Runnymede. *Stone* 5C **2**
Ruskin Dri. *Derr* 3G **11**
Russel St. *Staf* 2D **12**
Russetts, The. *Staf* 1F **19**
Rutherford Ct. *Staf T* 6A **8**
Rutherglen Clo. *Rug* 3B **22**
Rutland Av. *Rug* 6C **22**
Rydal Est. *Rug* 1E **23**
Rydall Ho. *Staf* 2F **13**
Rye Ct. *Staf* 6A **6**

S

Sabine St. *Staf* 4F **13**
Saddler Av. *Stone* 4E **3**
St Albans Rd. *Staf* 4E **7**
St Andrews Rd. *Staf* 6C **12**
St Anthonys Clo. *Rug* 4E **23**
St Augustine's Rd. *Rug* 6D **22**
St Austell Clo. *Staf* 5B **14**
St Barbara Ho. *Rug* 2D **22**
St Benedicts Dri. *L Hay* 5F **17**
St Bertellin Ct. Staf 5C 6
(off Holmcroft Rd.)
St Chads Clo. *L Hay* 6F **17**
St Chad's Clo. *Stone* 4E **3**
St Chad's Pl. *Staf* 2E **13**
St Chads Rd. *Ecc* 2A **4**
St Davids Rd. *Staf* 6D **12**
St Edwards Grn. *Rug* 5D **22**
St George Hill Ct. Staf 6D 6
(off Fancy Wlk.)
**ST GEORGE'S HOSPITAL
(STAFFORD).** **1F 13**

St George's Rd. *Staf* 3G **13**
St George's Rd. *Stone* 3D **2**
St Giles Gro. *Hau* 5D **10**
St Ives Clo. *Staf* 5B **14**
St James Cres. *Act T* 6H **19**
St John's Clo. *Rug* 4B **22**
St John's Rd. *Staf* 5D **12**
St John's Wlk. Staf 2G 13
(off Tithe Barn Rd., in three parts)
St Leonard's Av. *Staf* 4G **13**
St Martin's Pl. *Staf* 2E **13**
St Mary's Abbey 6F 17
St Mary's Ga. *Staf* 2E **13**
St Mary's Gro. *Staf* 2E **13**
St Mary's M. Staf 2E 13
(off St Mary's Pl.)
St Mary's Pl. *Staf* 2E **13**
St Marys Rd. *L Hay* 6F **17**
St Matthews Dri. *Derr* 3F **11**
St Mawes Clo. *Staf* 5B **14**
St Michael's Clo. *Penk* 3B **24**
St Michael's Clo. *Staf* 5C **14**
St Michaels Clo. *Stone* 3C **2**
St Michael's Ct. Stone 3C 2
(off Church St.)
St Michael's Dri. *Rug* 6A **22**
St Michael's Mt. *Stone* 5E **3**
St Michael's Rd. *Penk* 2B **24**
St Michael's Rd. *Rug* 6A **22**
St Michael's Sq. *Penk* 2B **24**
St Modwena Way. *Penk* 4C **24**
St Patrick's Pl. Staf 1E 13
(off St Patrick's St.)
St Patrick's St. *Staf* 1D **12**
St Paul's M. Rug 4E 23
(off St Pauls Rd.)
St Pauls Rd. *Rug* 4E **23**
St Peter's Clo. *Staf* 1F **19**
St Peter's Gdns. *Staf* 2F **19**
St Stephens Vw. *Gt Hay* 3D **16**
St Thomas La. *Tix* 2B **14**
St Thomas St. *Staf* 2G **13**
St Vincent Rd. *Stone* 3A **2**
Salcombe Av. *Staf* 5B **14**
Salisbury Dri. *Staf* 1H **13**
Salisbury Rd. *Staf* 1H **13**
Salmond Av. *Staf* 1H **13**
Salt Av. *Staf* 4E **13**
Salter St. *Staf* 2E **13**
Saltheath La. *Salt* 1C **8**
Saltings Res. Mobile Home Pk., The. *Staf* 3B **14**
Salt Rd. *Staf* 4E **13**
Salt Works La. *West* 1H **9**
Sandalwood Dri. *Staf* 6F **7**
Sandon M. *Staf* 5F **7**
Sandon Rd. *Hopt* 3F **7**
Sandon Rd. *Staf* 6E **7**
Sandown Cft. *Staf* 3D **12**
Sandringham Clo. *Staf* 5A **14**
Sandringham Rd. *Staf* 5A **14**
Sandyford Ct. *Staf* 6E **7**
Sandyford St. *Staf* 6E **7**
Sandy La. *Rug* 5D **22**
Sankey Cres. *Rug* 5D **22**
Saplings Clo. *Penk* 2C **24**
Saplings, The. *Penk* 2C **24**
Sarah Challinor Clo. *Rug* 4D **22**
Sash St. *Staf* 1D **12**
Savoureuse Dri. *Staf* 5G **13**
Sawpit La. *Broc* 4E **21**
Saxifrage Dri. *Stone* 5E **3**
Saxon Rd. *Penk* 3C **24**
Sayers Rd. *Staf* 4C **6**
Scholars Ga. *Rug* 6A **22**
School La. *Duns* 6F **19**
School La. *Gt Hay* 3D **16**
School La. *Staf* 2E **19**
School La. *Walt* 1D **20**
School La. Clo. *Staf* 2F **19**
School Pl. *Staf* 6E **7**
School Rd. *Ecc* 2A **4**
School Rd. *Rug* 2C **22**
Scotts Ho. Staf 6D 6
(off Marsh St.)
Seabrooke Rd. *Rug* 6A **22**
Searle Av. *Staf* 2C **12**
Seaton Av. *Staf* 5C **14**
Second Av. *Staf* 4B **6**
Seighford **5D 4**
Seighford Rd. *Seigh* 5E **5**
Selworthy Dri. *Staf* 1C **20**
Selwyn Ct. Ecc 1B 4
(off Castle St.)
Setterfield Way. *Rug* 6E **23**
Shaftsbury Rd. *Rug* 6D **22**
Shakespeare Rd. *Staf* 5C **12**
Shallowford M. *Staf* 6D **6**
Shannon Rd. *Staf* 1D **18**
Shardlow Clo. *Stone* 5E **3**
Sharnbrook Dri. *Rug* 2B **22**
Sharnbrook Gro. *Staf* 1A **20**
Shaw Gdns. *Staf* 6C **12**
Shawmans La. *Hau* 5A **10**
Shawms Crest. *Staf* 5A **14**
Shaws La. *Ecc* 2A **4**
Shebdon Clo. *Staf* 4B **6**
Sheep Fair. *Rug* 3D **22**
Shelley Clo. *L Hay* 5F **17**
Shelley Clo. *Staf* 6G **7**
Shelmore Clo. *Staf* 3B **6**
Shelsley Clo. *Penk* 2D **24**
Shenley Gro. *Staf* 1D **18**
Shephard Clo. *Gt Hay* 2D **16**
Shepherds Bush St. *Staf* 6E **7**
Shepherds Fold. *Staf* 1A **20**
Shepley Clo. *Stone* 4E **3**
Sherbrook Clo. *Broc* 4E **21**
Sheridan Cen. Staf 2E 13
(off Princes St.)
Sheridan Shop. Cen. Staf 2D 12
(off Mount St.)
Sheridan St. *Staf* 1F **13**
Sheridan Way. *Stone* 4F **3**
Sheriffs Way. *Ecc* 1A **4**
Sheringham Covert. *Staf* 1A **14**
Sheringham Dri. *Rug* 2A **22**
Sherwood Av. *Staf* 6E **13**
Shipston Rd. *Staf* 4B **14**
Shire Hall Gallery 2E 13
Shireoaks Dri. *Staf* 1A **20**
Shooting Butts Rd. *Rug* 3A **22**
Shrewsbury Mall. *Rug* 3E **23**
Shrewsbury Rd. *Staf* 4E **13**
Shrubbery, The. *Rug* 6G **23**
Shugborough Estate Watermill 5C 16
Shugborough Hall 3C 16
Shugborough Hall Servants Quarters' & County Mus. 4C 16
Shugborough Pk. 5B 16
Shugborough Pk. Farm Agricultural Mus. 5C 16
Shugborough Rd. *Rug* 1B **22**
Shugborough Ter. *L Hay* 5E **17**
Shut Heath **5A 10**
Sidings Rd. *Stone* 1A **2**
Sidings, The. *Stone* 3D **2**
Sidmouth Av. *Staf* 5B **14**
Sidney Av. *Staf* 6F **13**
Siemens Rd. *Staf* 4E **13**
Silk Mill M. Stone 3C 2
(off Lichfield St.)
Silkmore Cres. *Staf* 5G **13**
Silkmore La. *Staf* 1F **19**
(in two parts)
Silverthorn Way. *Staf* 6A **14**
Silvester Way. *Staf* 1C **20**
Simeon Way. *Stone* 5E **3**
Simpson Clo. *Staf* 4B **6**
Slaidburn Gro. *Staf* 6A **14**
Slessor Rd. *Staf* 6G **7**
Slitting Mill **5A 22**
Slitting Mill Rd. *Rug* 5A **22**
Small La. *Ecc* 1B **4**
Smallman St. *Staf* 1F **13**
Smithy La. *Hixon* 2H **17**
Smithy La. *Seigh* 5D **4**
Snead Clo. *Staf* 1A **14**
Sneydlands. *Rug* 3E **23**
Snow Hill. *Staf* 1E **13**
Snows Yd. *Staf* 1D **12**
Somerfield Arc. *Stone* 3C **2**
Somerset Av. *Rug* 6C **22**
Somerset Rd. *Staf* 6C **12**
Somervale. *Staf* 1A **20**
Somerville Sq. *Staf* 1F **19**
Somerville Ter. Rug 4D 22
(off Burnthill La.)
Southfields Clo. *Staf* 2D **18**
Southfields Rd. *Staf* 1D **18**
South St. *Staf* 2D **12**
South Walls. *Staf* 2E **13**
Southwell Est. *Ecc* 2B **4**
Sparrow Clo. *L Hay* 5F **17**
Speechly Dri. *Rug* 2C **22**
Speedwell Ri. *Staf* 6A **6**
Spencer Clo. *West* 1G **9**
Spenser Clo. *Staf* 5C **12**
Spinneyfields. *Staf* 2B **20**
Spode Av. *Staf* 3H **7**
(in two parts)
Spode Clo. *Stone* 6A **2**
Spreadoaks Dri. *Staf* 2B **20**
Sprengers Clo. *Penk* 2D **24**
Spring Banks Flats. *Staf* 5D **6**
Springfield Av. *Rug* 5E **23**
Springfield Ct. Staf 2E 19
(off Springfield Dri.)
Springfield Dri. *Staf* 2E **19**
Springfields Est. *Rug* 1C **22**
Springfields Rd. *Rug* 1C **22**
Spring Gdns. *Stone* 6C **2**
Springhill Ter. *Rug* 6E **23**
Springvale Ri. *Staf* 3D **6**
Springwood Dri. *Stone* 4F **3**
Spruce Wlk. *Rug* 1B **22**
Spruce Way. *Staf* 2C **12**
Square, The. *Derr* 3F **11**
Square, The. *Gt Hay* 3D **16**
Squirrel Wlk. *Staf* 3E **19**
Stables, The. *Gt Hay* 3D **16**
Stafford **2E 13**
Stafford Brook Rd. *Rug* 2A **22**
Stafford Castle 4A 12
Stafford Castle Vis. Cen. 4A 12
Stafford Clo. *Stone* 4C **2**
Stafford Ct. *Staf* 1B **14**
Stafford Crematorium. *Staf* 1B **14**
Stafford Rangers F.C. 5E 7
Stafford Rd. *Ecc* 2B **4**
Stafford Rd. *Penk* 1B **24**
Stafford Rd. *Stone* 4C **2**
Stafford Rd. *West* 1F **9**
Staffordshire County Showground 4D 8
STAFFORDSHIRE GENERAL HOSPITAL. 1G 13
Staffordshire Technology Pk. *Staf* 6A **8**
Stafford Sports Arena 5G 13
Stafford St. *Ecc* 1B **4**
Stafford St. *Staf* 2E **13**
Stafford St. *Stone* 3C **2**
Stafford Superbowl 1D 12
Stag Clo. *Rug* 3A **22**
Staines Ct. *Stone* 4E **3**
Stanford Clo. *Penk* 2B **24**
Stanway Ct. *Staf* 6F **7**
Station App. *Stone* 2B **2**
Station Rd. *Colw* 6F **17**
Station Rd. *Hau* 6A **10**
Station Rd. *Penk* 2B **24**
Station Rd. *Rug* 2D **22**
Station Rd. *Staf* 3D **12**
Station Rd. *Stone* 2B **2**
Steadman Cres. *Staf* 1E **19**
Steps Gdns. *Hau* 5C **10**
Stevenson Dri. *Staf* 6C **12**
Stile Clo. *Rug* 6E **23**
Stile Cop Rd. *Rug* 6C **22**
Stocking-Gate La. *Cot C* 4B **10**
Stockton La. *Staf* 6C **14**
Stone **3C 2**
Stone Bus. Pk. *Stone* 6D **2**
Stone Cross. *Penk* 2B **24**
Stone Enterprise Cen. *Stone* 6D **2**
Stonefield **1B 2**
Stonefield Ct. Stone 1B 2
(off Mount Rd.)
Stonefield M. *Stone* 2B **2**
Stonefield Sq. *Stone* 2C **2**
Stonehouse Rd. *Rug* 4A **22**
Stoneleigh Ct. *Hyde L* 2C **18**
Stonepine Clo. *Staf* 1A **20**
Stone Rd. *Ecc* 1B **4**
Stone Rd. *Staf* 6D **6**
Stone Rd. *Yar & Staf* 1B **6**
Stowe La. *Hixon* 1H **17**
Streamside Clo. *Penk* 3C **24**
Stretton Av. *Staf* 5B **6**
Stuart Clo. *Stone* 6B **2**
Stuart Clo. N. *Stone* 5B **2**
Stubbs Dri. *Stone* 4F **3**
Stychfields. *Staf* 4F **13**
Summerstreet La. *Stone* 1H **3**
Sundown Dri. *Staf* 5A **12**
Sunningdale. *Stone* 4C **2**
Sunningdale Dri. *Staf* 2A **14**
Surrey Clo. *Rug* 6C **22**
Surrey Rd. *Staf* 5C **12**
Sutherland Rd. *Stone* 4D **2**
Sutton Clo. *Rug* 6E **23**
Sutton Dri. *Staf* 1A **12**
Swallow Clo. *Rug* 2C **22**
Swallowdale. *Staf* 1B **20**
Swan Clo. *Rug* 6A **22**
Swan Clo. *Staf* 3C **12**
Sweetbriar Way. *Staf* 1A **20**
Swinburne Clo. *Staf* 5C **12**
Sycamore Cres. *Rug* 6F **23**
Sycamore Dri. *Hixon* 2G **17**
Sycamore La. *Staf* 6B **12**
Sycamore Rd. *Stone* 3D **2**
Sylvan Way. *Staf* 2A **20**

T

Talbot Rd. *Rug* 6E **23**
Talbot Rd. *Staf* 4E **13**
Talbot St. *Rug* 4E **23**
Tallpines. *Staf* 6A **14**
Tamar Gro. *Staf* 5B **12**
Tannery Clo. *Rug* 3E **23**
Tannery Wlk. *Stone* 5C **2**
Taplin Clo. *Staf* 4D **6**
Tarragona Dri. *Staf* 5G **13**
Tasman Dri. *Staf* 6H **7**
Taverners Dri. *Stone* 5F **3**
Tavistock Av. *Staf* 4B **14**
Taylor's La. *Rug* 3D **22**
Taylor Wlk. *Staf* 6C **12**
Tedder Rd. *Staf* 6G **7**
Teddesley Rd. *Bed* 6A **20**
Teddesley Rd. *Penk* 2B **24**
Telegraph St. *Staf* 4E **13**
Telford Clo. *Stone* 5E **3**
Telford Dri. *Toll I* 3F **7**
Templars Way. *Penk* 3C **24**
Ten Butts Cres. *Staf* 2F **19**
Tenby Dri. *Staf* 4F **7**
Tennyson Rd. *Staf* 5B **12**
Tenterbanks. *Staf* 2D **12**
Teveray Dri. *Penk* 4C **24**
Thackeray Wlk. *Staf* 6C **12**
Thames Way. *Staf* 5B **12**
Thirlmere Way. *Staf* 6E **13**
Thistle Clo. *Rug* 2B **22**
Thomas Av. *Staf* 2B **12**
Thomas Av. *Stone* 5E **3**
Thompson Clo. *Staf* 6C **12**
Thompson Rd. *Rug* 6B **22**
Thorn Clo. *Rug* 5F **23**
Thorneyfields La. *Staf* 5A **12**
Thorneyfields La. *Staf & Hyde L* 6A **12**
Tilcon Av. *Staf* 3A **14**
Tildesley Clo. *Penk* 3B **24**
Tilling Dri. *Stone* 4B **2**
Tillington **5C 6**
Tillington St. *Staf* 6D **6**
Timberfield Rd. *Staf* 1C **12**
Tipping St. *Staf* 2E **13**
Tithe Barn Ct. *Staf* 1G **13**
Tithebarn Rd. *Rug* 2D **22**
Tithe Barn Rd. *Staf* 2G **13**
Tiverton Av. *Staf* 5B **14**
Tixall **3H 15**
Tixall Ct. *Tix* 2A **16**
Tixall M. *Tix* 2H **15**
Tixall Rd. *Staf & Tix* 2G **13**
Toft, The **6A 18**
Tolldish **1F 17**
Tolldish La. *Gt Hay* 2E **17**
Tollgate Bus. Cen. *Staf* 4F **7**
Tollgate Dri. *Toll I* 4F **7**
Tollgate Ind. Est. *Staf* 3F **7**
(Brindley Clo.)
Tollgate Ind. Est. *Staf* 4F **7**
(Tollgate Dri.)
Top Rd. *Act T* 6H **19**
Torridge Dri. *Staf* 5B **12**
Torrington Av. *Staf* 5C **14**
Tourist Info. Cen. 2E 13
(Stafford)
Towers Bus. Pk. *Rug* 6G **23**
Toy Clo. *Rug* 3C **22**
Trenchard Av. *Staf* 1G **13**
Trent Bus. Pk. *Rug* 2E **23**
Trent Clo. *Gt Hay* 3D **16**
Trent Clo. *Staf* 1F **19**
Trent La. *Gt Hay* 3D **16**
Trent Rd. *Stone* 2A **2**
Trent Valley Trad. Est. *Rug* 1E **23**
Trent Vw. Clo. *Rug* 5F **23**
Trent Wlk. *Ing* 4H **9**
Trevelyan's Grn. *Staf* 3C **6**
Trinity Dri. *Stone* 2B **2**

Trinity Fields 3C 6
Trinity Gorse. Staf 3B 6
Trinity Ri. Staf 3B 6
Trinity Rd. Ecc 2A 4
Trubshaw Clo. L Hay 5G 17
Truro Way. Staf 4B 14
Trussell Clo. Act T 6G 19
Tudor Clo. Stone 5B 2
Tudor Ri. Staf 3C 6
Tudor Way. Staf 4B 12
Tullis Clo. Staf 3C 12
Tunley St. Stone 2B 2
Tunnicliffe Dri. Rug 3C 22
Turney Gro. Staf 5C 12
Turnhill Clo. Staf 1C 18
Twemlow Clo. Derr 3F 11
Tylecote Cres. Gt Hay 3D 16
Tyler Gro. Stone 4A 2
Tyria Way. Staf 5G 13

U

Ullswater Dri. Stone 4F 3
Ullswater Ho. Staf 1E 19 (off Merrivale Rd.)
Underwood Clo. Staf 3C 6
University Ct. Staf T 6A 8
Upfield Way. Rug 2B 22
Uplands Clo. Penk 1B 24
Uplands Grn. Rug 6C 22
Uplands Rd. Staf 1D 18
Uplands, The. Gt Hay 3D 16
Upmeadows Dri. Staf 4B 12
Up. Brook St. Rug 4D 22
Up. Cross Rd. Rug 5D 22
Upton Pl. Rug 2C 22
Usulwall Clo. Ecc 2A 4
Uttoxeter Rd. Stone 5F 3

V

Vale Gdns. Penk 4B 24
Vale Ri. Penk 3B 24
Valley Rd. Stone 4C 2
Varden Ct. Rug 3D 22
Vardon Clo. Staf 2A 14
Vaughan Way. Staf 4B 12
Verdon Clo. Penk 4D 24
Verulam Ct. Staf 4E 7
Verulam Rd. Staf 4E 7
Verwood Clo. Staf 1A 14
Vicarage Clo. Ecc 1A 4
Vicarage Way. Hixon 1H 17
Vicarage Way. Staf 4D 12
Vicars Cft. Rug 2E 23
Victoria Pk. Staf 2D 12 (off Tenterbanks)
Victoria Rd. Staf 2D 12
Victoria Sq. Staf 2D 12
Victoria St. Staf 1E 13
Victoria St. Stone 2C 2
Victoria Ter. Staf 6E 7
Victoria Way. Staf 2C 20
Victor St. Stone 2B 2
Village Gdns. Staf 6D 14
Village, The. Walt 6D 14 (in two parts)
Vine Clo. Hixon 2G 17
Virginia Av. Staf 5G 13

W

Walden Av. Staf 5D 6
Walhouse Dri. Penk 4C 24
Walland Gro. Staf 1B 12
Walnut Ct. Rug 6A 22
Walnut Crest. Hixon 2H 17
Walton 4C 2
Waltonbury Clo. Walt 1D 20
Walton Cross. Stone 4C 2
Walton Grange. Stone 4C 2
Walton Ind. Est. Stone 5C 2 (Beacon Dri.)
Walton Ind. Est. Stone 6B 2 (Beacon Rd.)
Walton La. Broc 2E 21
Walton Lodge. Walt 1D 20
Walton Mead Clo. Staf 6D 14
Walton-on-the-Hill 1D 20
Walton Way. Stone 4B 2
Warm Cft. Stone 4E 3
Warrens La. Staf 5B 6
Warwick Rd. Staf 5H 13
Washington Dri. Staf 5G 13
Waterbrook Clo. Penk 4B 24
Water Eaton La. Penk 4A 24
Waterford Ct. Staf 6G 7 (off Elworthy Clo.)
Waterside. Rug 6E 23
Waterside Bus. Pk. Rug 5F 23
Watersmeet Ct. Stone 5E 3
Water St. Staf 2E 13
Watery La. Hau 6D 10
Watkiss Dri. Rug 3C 22
Watson Clo. Rug 1C 22
Wattfield Clo. Rug 6A 22
Wattles La. Act T 5H 19
Watts Clo. Staf 5B 12
Wat Tyler Clo. Rug 1C 22
Waverley Gdns. Rug 2A 22
Wayfield Dri. Staf 3D 6
Weaver Dri. Staf 5B 12
Weavers La. Stone 5D 2
Wedgewood Av. Stone 5A 2
Wedgwood Rd. Hopt 3H 7
Weeping Cross 5C 14
Weeping Cross. Staf 6B 14
Wellington Clo. Staf 6E 7
Wellington Dri. Rug 4E 23
Wells Dri. Staf 6C 14
Wellyards Clo. West 1H 9
Wentworth Dri. Staf 2A 14
Wesley Dri. Stone 5E 3
Westbridge Pk. Sports Cen. 3C 2
Westbury Hayes. Staf 5A 12
W. Butts Rd. Rug 3A 22
West Clo. Staf 2G 13
West Clo. Stone 4B 2
W. Douglas Rd. Staf 6G 7
Western Downs 4B 12
Western Springs Rd. Rug 2C 22
Western Vw. Rug 2C 22 (off Fernwood Dri.)
Westhead Av. Staf 1G 13
Westhorpe. Staf 4D 12
Westminster Clo. Staf 5A 14
Weston Bank. Hopt 3D 8
Weston Rd. Staf 2G 13
Weston-upon-Trent 1H 9
West Way. Staf 4C 12
W. Way Grn. Staf 5C 12
Westwood Dri. Penk 3C 24
Wetherall Clo. Rug 2C 22
Wharf Ho. Rug 3E 23 (off Bryans La.)
Wharf Rd. Rug 5D 22
Wheatcroft Clo. Penk 3B 24
Wheelhouse Rd. Rug 5F 23
Whimster Sq. Staf 5A 12
Whiston Rd. Penk 3A 24
Whitby Clo. Staf 6C 12
Whitebridge La. Stone 1A 2
Whitebridge La. Ind. Est. Stone 1A 2
Whitecross 4A 10
White Lion St. Staf 3E 13
Whitemill La. Stone 4B 2
White Oaks. Staf 2A 20
Whitgreave Ct. Staf 6D 6
Whitgreave La. Gt Bri 1E 5
Whitgreave La. Rug 6D 22
Whittingham Dri. Staf 5B 12
Whitworth La. Rug 2A 22
Widecombe Av. Staf 6C 14
Wildwood 6A 14
Wildwood Dri. Staf 6A 14
Wildwood Ga. Staf 1B 20
Wildwood Lawns. Staf 6A 14
Wildwood Shop. Cen. Staf 1B 20 (off Wildwood Ga.)
Wilke's Wood. Staf 3H 5
William Morris Ct. Rug 1C 22
Williams Clo. Staf 2B 12
Williams Ct. Staf 4F 7
Willoughby Clo. Penk 4C 24
Willowbrook. Derr 3G 11
Willow Clo. Penk 4C 24
Willow Clo. Staf 1D 20
Willowmoor. Staf 2E 19
Willow Rd. Stone 4D 2
Willows, The. Rug 6A 22
Willows, The. Stone 5D 2
Willow Wlk. Stone 4D 2
Wilmore Ct. Hopt 2B 8
Wilmore Hill La. Hopt 2A 8
Wilson Keys Ct. Rug 2D 22
Winchester Ct. Staf 1A 20
Windermere Ho. Staf 2F 13
Windsor Clo. Stone 6B 2
Windsor Rd. Staf 6H 13
Winsford Cres. Staf 1C 20
Winstanley Clo. Rug 2C 22
Winstanley Pl. Rug 2C 22
Wiscombe Av. Penk 2C 24
Within La. Hopt 1A 8
Witney Rd. Staf 4B 14
Wogan St. Staf 6E 7
Wolgarston Way. Penk 4C 24
Wolseley Clo. Colw 6G 17
Wolseley Rd. Rug 1C 22
Wolseley Rd. Staf 2A 14
Wolverhampton Rd. Penk 5A 24
Wolverhampton Rd. Staf 4E 13
Woodbank La. Penk 1D 24
Woodberry Clo. Staf 3F 19
Woodcock Rd. Rug 3B 22
Woodcote, The. Staf 6A 14
Wood Cres. Staf 5B 6
Wood Cres. Stone 6B 2
Woodheyes Lawns. Rug 3B 22
Woodhouse La. Hau 5A 10
Woodings Yd. Staf 3E 13 (off Bailey St.)
Woodlands Av. Stone 3A 2
Woodlands Clo. Staf 3C 6
Woodlands Clo. Stone 3A 2
Woodlands Rd. Staf 4B 6
Wood La. Stone 6B 2
Woodleyes Cres. Staf 1B 20
Woodside Clo. L Hay 5F 17
Woodstock Rd. Staf 4B 14
Woodtherne Clo. Penk 3C 24
Woodthorne Clo. Rug 2B 22
Wood Vw. Rug 6E 23
Wootton Dri. Staf 4A 6
Wordsworth Av. Staf 5B 12
Wrenswood. Staf 1A 20
Wright St. Staf 6E 7
Wulfad Ct. Stone 4E 3
Wulfric Clo. Penk 3D 24
Wycherwood Gdns. Staf 2B 20

Y

Yarlet Cft. Staf 5D 6
Yarnfield La. Stone 3A 2
Yelverton Av. Staf 5B 14
Yew Tree Clo. Derr 3G 11
Yew Tree Ct. Staf 3E 19
Yew Tree Rd. Rug 6E 23
York Rd. Staf 5G 13
York St. Stone 1C 2
Young Av. Staf 5C 6